TREASURES OF THE ORIENTAL MUSEUM
DURHAM UNIVERSITY

Seek knowledge even as far as China

TREASURES OF
THE ORIENTAL MUSEUM
DURHAM UNIVERSITY

EDITED BY CRAIG BARCLAY, RACHEL GROCKE AND HELEN ARMSTRONG

PHOTOGRAPHY BY KATE WEIGHTMAN

 Durham University

 THIRD MILLENNIUM PUBLISHING, LONDON

 Designated as an Outstanding Collection

 Arts & Humanities Research Council

 Supported by The National Lottery® through the Heritage Lottery Fund

 heritage lottery fund

[title page]
Chinese jade boulder carved in the form of a mountain landscape (no. 7).

Right: detail of Japanese ivory carving of a weaver and his family (no. 28).

TREASURES OF THE ORIENTAL MUSEUM, DURHAM UNIVERSITY

© Durham University and Third Millennium Publishing Limited

Autumn Glory by Chao Mei © Muban Foundation

First published in 2010 by
Third Millennium Publishing Limited,
a subsidiary of Third Millennium Information Limited.

2–5 Benjamin Street
London
United Kingdom
EC1M 5QL
www.tmiltd.com

ISBN 978 1 906507 35 0

Edited by Craig Barclay, Rachel Grocke and Helen Armstrong
Photography by Kate Weightman
Designed by Susan Pugsley
Production by Bonnie Murray

Reprographics by Studio Fasoli, Italy
Printed by Gorenjski Tisk, Slovenia

NOTE ON DATING CONVENTIONS
In keeping with the practice adopted in
the Oriental Museum's display galleries,
all dates in this volume are given using
the 'Common Era' system. BCE (before
Common Era) corresponds to BC; CE
(Common Era) to AD.

MAPS
The names shown and the designations
used on the maps in this book do not
imply official endorsement or acceptance
by Durham University.

Contents

FOREWORD

The Oriental Museum is one of Durham University's, and indeed the region's, real treasures.

I recall that I was left somewhat dumbstruck upon arriving at the museum for the first time to discover such a fascinating collection of exotic marvels tucked away in the leafy woodland on Elvet Hill.

On that day I only had twenty minutes, but it was the best twenty minutes I've spent in a long time. I have now made it my duty as Durham University Chancellor to urge everyone who has yet to visit the Oriental Museum to drop everything and go at once. It's that good.

This volume provides a fitting showcase to an intriguing and alluring collection of art and artefacts. I hope you enjoy the book and seize the first opportunity to visit the museum.

Bill Bryson

Left: Chinese bowl from the Song Dynasty (no. 3).

ACKNOWLEDGEMENTS AND CONTRIBUTORS

The production of this volume would not have been possible without the unflinching support of Durham University, the Friends of the Oriental Museum, and the contributors who have so generously devoted their time and not inconsiderable energies to researching and writing the individual essays contained within its covers.

Special thanks are also due to Chris Orton and David Hume of the Geography Department's Design and Imaging Unit for producing the splendid maps; to Caitlin McInnis for undertaking much of the original project research; to Julia Oliver and Lyn Gatland for providing proof-reading and office support; to Jon Purcell, John Hall and Sheila Hingley for supporting our original vision; and to the University Museums' front-of-house team for their endless patience and understanding. We also owe a great debt of gratitude to Joel Burden, Susan Pugsley and the team at TMI for taking our dreams and turning them into a reality.

But most of all we would like to express our thanks to the many donors whose kindness has allowed us to develop such wonderful collections. Without their boundless curiosity, exquisite taste and generosity of spirit there would be no Oriental Museum.

BOOK CONTRIBUTORS

Helen Armstrong, Durham University Museums
Dr Ralph Austin, Chairman of the Friends of the Oriental Museum
Prof John Baines, University of Oxford
Craig Barclay, Durham University Museums
Diana de Bellaigue, National Museums of Scotland
Prof Robin Coningham, Durham University
Robert Cumming, University College London
Christopher Davis, Durham University
Dr Aidan Dodson, Bristol University
Embroiderers' Guild volunteers, North East Region
Dr Karen Exell, The Manchester Museum, University of Manchester
Dr Emma Gilberthorpe, University of East Anglia
Rachel Grocke, Durham University Museums
Dr John Hall, potter, formerly Durham University
Sophie Harrison, The Art Fund
Dr Weimin He, University of Oxford
Lewis Hill, University of Hull
Kathryn Jacques, Durham University
Dr Frances Larson, Durham University
Jane McAdam Freud, artist

Dr Johannes Haubold, Durham University
Dipti Khera, Columbia University
Kirsty McCarrison, Durham University
Caitlin McInnis, Fairhaven Originals Gallery, WA, USA
Dr Simon Mills, Durham University
Dr Mohammad Javad Nateghpour, University of Tehran, Iran
Prof Nick Pearce, University of Glasgow
Prof Keith Pratt, Durham University
Dr Sarah Price, Durham University
John Ruffle, former Curator of the Oriental Museum
Prof Hans Schneider, Rijksmuseum for Antiquities, Leiden
Sonika Soni, City Palace Museum, Udaipur, India
Dr Janet Starkey, Durham University
Don Starr, Durham University
Prof F Richard Stephenson, Durham University
Mrinalini Venkateswaran, City Palace Museum, Udaipur, India
Dr Toby Wilkinson, Cambridge University
Ifan Williams, collector and author
Dr Penny Wilson, Durham University
Mr Hideaki Yokohama, Consul for Cultural Affairs, Consulate of Japan in Edinburgh

Left: detail of Chinese terracotta model of a polo player from the Tang Dynasty (no. 2).

INTRODUCTION

'If you have never been to Durham, go there at once. Take my car. It's wonderful.'

BILL BRYSON

NOTES FROM A SMALL ISLAND (1995)

Durham University's Oriental Museum is one of North East England's cultural gems, boasting a world-class collection of 23,500 items relating to Egypt, China, India, Japan and the other great cultures of Asia and Islamic North Africa. Founded in 1960 primarily as a resource to support the University's teaching and research agendas, it has developed over the past half-century into a world-class institution which combines its traditional academic role with a commitment to making its collections accessible to all.

THE SCHOOL OF ORIENTAL STUDIES

'The Orient' is not an area with defined geographical boundaries and the term can mean widely differing things to different people, from a very narrow definition relating to East Asia, to a much wider concept stretching beyond the boundaries of Asia into the Near and Middle East. In the case of the Oriental Museum, the definition is a wide one indeed, and the collections cover an enormous area ranging from North Africa right through to South East Asia (see world map below). This coverage is a legacy of the origins of the Oriental Museum, which is in turn inextricably linked to the story of oriental language teaching at Durham University.

The study of languages and literature of the ancient Middle East formed part of the theology curriculum from the University's foundation in 1832, with courses in Biblical Hebrew, and later Aramaic, being offered as part of the theology degree. Teaching expanded in the 1920s, when the distinguished Islamicist Alfred Guillaume developed unique courses in both modern and classical Arabic.

In 1941 Thomas W Thacker was appointed as Professor of Hebrew and Oriental Languages. During the war years Thacker was involved in developing a Near Eastern intelligence section within

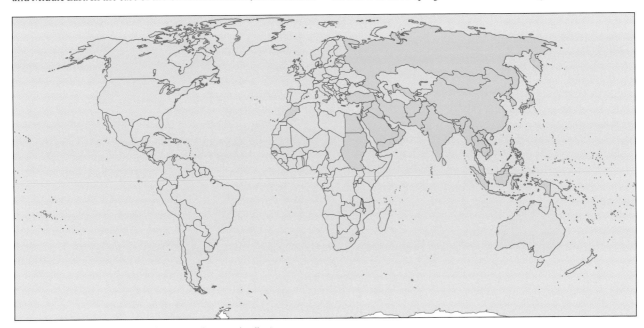

World map highlighting the origins of the Oriental Museum's collections.

Left: the city of Durham.

the Foreign Office and this experience left him keenly aware of the need to train more linguists proficient in the modern languages of the Near and Far East. On his return to Durham after the war Thacker proposed the expansion of teaching of both Arabic and Hebrew. Fortuitously, the Scarborough Commission – which had been set up to review the teaching of Oriental languages in British Universities – recommended that Durham be selected as one of five universities in which special facilities should be developed for this purpose. As a result, a new School of Oriental Studies was established in Durham in 1951, with Professor Thacker as its Director.

The early emphasis was to build on Durham's existing strengths and concentrate on the languages and cultures of the Near East and posts were soon established in Egyptology and Turkish, Persian Studies and Assyriology. The Turkish post also allowed the School to extend its interests into the Turkic speaking republics of the USSR. As well as ordinary students, Durham lecturers were soon heavily involved in training intelligence officers, diplomats and military personnel, with the salary of the Arabic lecturer being paid for some years by the War Office and Air Ministry.

From the outset Professor Thacker was adamant that the teaching of languages must be supported by an understanding of material culture, arguing that, 'An Oriental School which aims to teach the cultural background of the oriental peoples must have a museum at its disposal.' Not only was there no such museum in Durham, in Thacker's opinion there were no adequate collections anywhere in the North East. He therefore determined to create his own museum.

THE NORTHUMBERLAND COLLECTION

By happy coincidence at this time Hugh Percy, 10th Duke of Northumberland, was seeking a buyer for the family collection of Ancient Egyptian and Mesopotamian antiquities. Algernon Percy, the 4th Duke, had been an avid and informed collector of Egyptian antiquities in the 19th century, acquiring one of the finest private collections in the UK and displaying it at the family home, Alnwick Castle. This was further enriched by the collection of Henry Percy, eldest son of the 7th Duke, who collected antiquities from Mesopotamia and Asia Minor.

Prior to the Second World War the collection had been sent to the British Museum for conservation. It was never unpacked,

being sent instead into safe storage for the duration of the War. The Duke informed Professor Thacker of his intention to sell the collection and Thacker quickly began to lobby the University to support its acquisition. Durham was not the only interested party, with the British Museum itself and the Brooklyn Museum in New York also submitting bids. What Thacker described as 'a lively struggle' ensued. Happily for Durham the Duke was keen for the collection to stay in the North East and with the support of the University and a generous donation from Dr and Mrs HN Spalding, an agreement was reached.

Thacker's case to the University for the purchase of the collection, numbering more than 2,500 objects of the highest quality, makes fascinating reading. One of Thacker's arguments for the collection to come to Durham vividly reflects the concerns of post-war Britain:

'in these days of aerial warfare egyptological collections are not immune from destruction … because of the menace from the air it is unwise to allow our treasures to become too centralised or always deposit them in towns which could become military targets. Durham is not so placed and is never likely to be.'

He also rather optimistically claimed that the ongoing expenses for the care and curation of the collection would be negligible. The only real expenditure that he envisaged was that 'perhaps an extra cleaner would be required' and a few cases might be needed for some of the smaller objects.

The collections arrived in Durham in August of 1950 and were housed initially in Hatfield College. Two rooms were put aside, one for display and another as a store and work-room. In the annual reports of the School at this time, Thacker proudly referred to this 'museum', though for reasons of security the rooms were always locked and the collections could only be viewed by appointment. By 1954 these rooms became increasingly overcrowded as other acquisitions arrived and in the summer of 1956 a fire broke out in the building where the collections were housed. The collections were saved but the exhibition space was badly water-damaged and the artefacts had to be placed in temporary storage whilst the area was redecorated. Thacker's ambitions were further undermined when Hatfield then requested the return of the storage space to allow them to create new accommodation for the Master of the

Elvet Hill House (photo courtesy of the Fogg-Elliot family).

College. Thacker consequently lost half of his floor-space. The collections had again to be packed up and placed in storage in what had hitherto been the exhibition gallery, effectively putting an end to the nascent museum.

CHINA AND INDIA

Eager to extend the reach of the School beyond the Near and Middle East, in 1952 Professor Thacker had secured a further donation from Dr and Mrs Spalding to support the establishment of two new lectureships: one in Indian Religions and Philosophies and the other in Chinese Philosophy (later expanded to incorporate Chinese languages). This expansion opened the way for the acquisition of artefacts from East and South Asia.

Much of the credit for the development of the Chinese collections must go to Raymond Dawson, who was appointed to the Chinese lecturer post. In 1953, in celebration of the Queen's coronation, the School hosted an exhibition of Chinese bronzes lent by Mr AEK Cull. Dawson curated the exhibition and conducted visitors around the displays, receiving considerable support from Perceval Yetts, Professor of Chinese Art at the Courtauld Institute of Art, who had written a catalogue on Cull's collection in 1939. It was to prove a significant collaboration, and in later accounts Dawson gave much of the credit for the birth of the Oriental Museum to Yetts and his support.

In 1954 Dawson organised a follow-up exhibition of Chinese textiles and books at Cosin's Library on Palace Green. Further exhibitions followed as other new acquisitions arrived, with a display of Chinese artefacts held at Elvet Hill House attracting a significant amount of press interest. These exhibitions and the continuing influence of Yetts appear to have stimulated considerable interest among potential donors and Dawson happily proved adept at negotiating agreements with major benefactors such as Malcolm MacDonald and Sir Charles Hardinge. Other important early acquisitions included a fine collection of Gandharan sculpture and the Marshall collection of almost 5,000 photographs of Indian architecture and sculpture.

MALCOLM MACDONALD

Malcolm MacDonald first visited the Far East in 1929 when, as a recently elected MP, he attended an international conference in Kyoto. Already a connoisseur and collector of English pottery, MacDonald's post-conference travels through Korea, China and Manchuria opened his eyes to the wonders of Chinese ceramics. It was on this visit that he made his first purchases, including two Ming Dynasty lions that were ultimately destined to become part of the Oriental Museum's collection.

In 1946 MacDonald returned to the Far East to take up the post of Governor General of Malaya and Singapore, later becoming Commissioner General for South East Asia. Although based in Singapore, MacDonald travelled extensively throughout the region, providing him with ample opportunity to collect Chinese ceramics in earnest. In 1955 he was appointed as High Commissioner to India. Reluctant to move his exceptional collection from his home in Singapore to India, MacDonald approached Peter Vaughan, Director of the dealers John Sparks Ltd, to help him find a museum in the UK to which he might lend the collection. It was Vaughan who put MacDonald in touch with Raymond Dawson.

The MacDonald collection arrived in Durham in 1956, initially on the basis of a 5-year loan agreement. A total of 235 objects were shipped from Singapore, with a further small selection travelling north from MacDonald's London home. MacDonald did not however stop collecting and, almost as soon as the collection arrived in Durham, he began to add additional pieces with the idea of creating a comprehensive teaching collection from prehistory to the end of the Imperial Period.

ELVET HILL HOUSE

As the School of Oriental Studies expanded, it swiftly outgrew the space that had initially been allocated to it. It found a new home in 1955, when the University acquired Elvet Hill House, a large country house standing in its own grounds to the south of the city, and adapted it to create teaching spaces and a library.

Within the confines of Elvet Hill House the School continued to thrive and grow, with an expanding library and ever-growing collection of objects competing for space with new academic staff. A room was set aside to house exhibitions, and other objects from the collection were displayed in showcases sited on the landings of the main staircase. These arrangements were however far from satisfactory: only a fraction of the collections now owned by or on loan to the department could be displayed and the Northumberland Collection remained at Hatfield, a mile away.

GENESIS OF THE MUSEUM

While Thacker's original plan for a museum had been solely focused on the needs of departmental teaching and research, the success of Dawson's exhibitions convinced him of the need to create a museum on a grander scale. This would be attractive to

Image of museum exterior in the 1960s.

Level 3 of the Oriental Museum in 1960. The figure in the centre is Professor Thacker (photo courtesy of Dr David Marshall).

potential donors, be a prestigious asset to the University and create a cultural amenity for the region. An approach was accordingly made to the Lisbon-based Gulbenkian Foundation and in 1957 it agreed to donate £60,000 to fund the first stage of the creation of what was to be known as the Gulbenkian Museum of Oriental Art and Archaeology. The architects appointed to build the museum were a local Middlesbrough firm, Philip R Middleton and Partner.

Although the museum was to be open to the public, the emphasis remained very much on teaching and research. Study-rooms and a library accordingly featured prominently in the original plans, along with the more usual offices, stores, photographic studio and workroom. As a teaching centre, it was considered to be essential that the new museum was built close to the School of Oriental Studies. A bold decision was therefore made to construct the building on the steep incline to the side of Elvet Hill House. The architects faced up to this challenge by creating a highly unusual design for the interior of the museum, with the entrance at the highest point, opposite the main door of the house, and three open-plan galleries positioned below this

Photograph of the moon-rock sample (photo courtesy of NASA).

Model of proposed 1980s extension, designed by Trevor Horne ARIBA.

level, following the contour of the hill. The three galleries were intended to hold Egyptian, Middle Eastern and Far Eastern objects respectively, with the large back wall designed for the display of the museum's Chinese Imperial curtains. Building work began in 1958 and was completed in the autumn of 1959. The various collections were transferred from Hatfield College and Elvet Hill House in late 1959 and the displays created over a six-month period before the official opening in May 1960.

One of the highlights of the original display was the Hardinge collection. As early as 1953, Professor Thacker had been able to record in the Annual Report for the School of Oriental Studies that 'a famous collector', had agreed to donate his collection to the School. This donor was Sir Charles Hardinge, whose collection of almost 3,000 Chinese objects was particularly strong in the areas of jade and other hardstones. Hardinge had intended the collection to come to the museum on this death. However, in 1959 he suffered an accident which compelled him to give up his house and move into a nursing home. He therefore asked the School to accept his gift prematurely and, at very short notice, the entire collection (including furniture, pictures, five clocks and a number of display cases) had to be transported to Durham. From the University's perspective, the timing could not have been better, for, whilst the museum building had been completed, its cases had yet to be filled. It was accordingly possible to incorporate Hardinge's fantastic collection into the displays, which opened to the public in May 1960.

Raymond Dawson had been offered the post of Keeper of the Gulbenkian Museum but he chose instead to return to his academic career and focus on the teaching of Chinese language, moving shortly afterwards to Oxford. The Indian specialist Philip Rawson was appointed to the post instead, although as his specialism was not at the time very well represented in the collection he was given the lesser title of Curator, and was subject to a committee of Honorary Keepers drawn from the School. Initially public opening hours were very limited, being 2.15–5pm on Mondays, Wednesdays and Fridays. Even so, around 100 visitors a week found their way to the museum.

If the number of members of the public visiting the museum during the 1960s generally remained modest, it was to experience a moment of glory as the decade came to an end. Given the richness of its collections however, it is perhaps ironic that the thing for which the museum remains most famous locally is not an oriental object at all but a moon-rock! In October 1969 a small fragment of rock collected on the first moon landing

Right: The museum's famous Chinese bed, part of the displays in the Marvels of China Gallery (photo by Lee Dobson).

was sent to Durham University for analysis by scientists in the Earth Sciences Department. Prior to this the rock was put on show at the Oriental Museum for two days. It created a sensation: 12,000 people queued for up to five hours to see the rock and the museum was forced to open until 8.30pm on the second day to accommodate the thousands of locals who came to see it. Museum staff members still regularly encounter local residents who say that the only time they remember visiting the museum was to queue to see the moon-rock.

EVOLUTION AND DEVELOPMENT

It should not be forgotten that the museum as it stands today was designed as the first phase of a much larger project. Even at the time of the opening in May 1960 the museum was far too small to allow the display of the whole collection. During the planning and construction phase attempts had been made to increase the available display space within the building, with plans for a

library being abandoned in favour of additional display space for the Egyptian collections, and the walls of the seminar room being lined with cases of Near Eastern material. Even this was not enough however and space remained at a premium.

This should have represented no more than a temporary inconvenience. The grand plan was for this building to form the first of three matching units which would wrap around Elvet Hill House. The architects Middletons drew up plans for the second phase of the museum in 1963. The second unit was to be linked to the existing museum via a glass walkway and a Japanese garden was to have been created between the two. It was envisaged that at a later date a third matching building would be constructed further round the hill. However, funding for the second phase of building was not forthcoming and the plans had to be shelved. At one point in the late 1960s consideration was given to converting the museum's store into a fourth large gallery, but again these plans were never carried out. In the 1970s the plans were again

Oriental Art from Durham University and Eton College, on display in the Utsunomiya Museum of Art, Japan (photo by Craig Barclay).

revisited. Some limited funding was secured, but it unfortunately proved insufficient to allow work to commence on the second phase of the museum project.

In 1981 it was decided to reconsider the problem. By this time the museum's function was much more public-facing and the disadvantages of its hidden entrance were becoming obvious. The Keeper at this time, John Ruffle, took the decision to hold a national competition in conjunction with the RIBA for a completely new solution. The competition was launched in July 1982. In all, 126 entries were received, from which six were selected to proceed to a second stage. These six were asked to produce more detailed proposals and the winning proposal, by Horne and Malcolm, a group of young, London-based architects, was announced in July 1983.

The proposed extension consisted of an arrangement of side galleries around a central atrium. The design was created to blend with and link to the old building, while also providing a new public entrance on the main road. Other facilities included a lecture theatre in the basement and a café area at the new entrance. Disappointingly, despite a very active campaign led by museum staff and the newly-formed Friends of the Oriental Museum, it

still proved impossible to raise the sums of money required for a new building. A decision was accordingly made to develop a new gallery within the existing shell of the museum, rather than build a completely new extension. Heritage Lottery Funding was secured and in 2000 the museum closed for a period of nine months to facilitate the creation of a new mezzanine floor. Fresh displays highlighting the Chinese collections were then installed in the new gallery – *Marvels of China* – whilst other improvements included the construction of a temporary exhibition room, the building of an education room, the installation of full disabled access and the opening of a new cafeteria.

In 2008 the quality of the museum's collections of Egyptology and of Chinese art and archaeology were formally recognised by the granting of 'Designated Collection' status by the Museums, Libraries and Archives Council (MLA). This prestigious award – which is restricted to collections assessed to be of national or international importance – is hard won and represents the highest accolade available to institutions outside the national

Right: New Egyptology displays, opened to the public in 2009.

20

View of the Oriental Museum galleries in 2008 (Photo by Lee Dobson).

museums sector. A further reminder of the pre-eminence of the collections was received in 2008, when the museum was invited (in collaboration with Eton College) to take 150 pieces from its Egyptology collection on a multi-venue tour of Japan. The resulting exhibition, entitled *Oriental Art from Durham University and Eton College*, was sponsored by *Tokyo Shimbun* newspaper. During the course of its nine-month tour of Japan it visited Utsunomiya, Atami, Hamamatsu, Nagoya, Kobe and Tokyo and was seen by 185,692 visitors. This represented a marvellous opportunity to raise the profile of Durham University in Japan, and also brought significant financial benefits to the museum, in the form of a £60,000 hire fee.

The income raised from the Japanese tour has been directed towards improving the public galleries. As a first phase of this programme a new Egyptology gallery has been created to house some of the highlights of the collection. This has allowed many of the museum's finest pieces to be re-interpreted in cases which have been fully refurbished to meet modern conservation standards. LED lighting (which emits no ultraviolet radiation) has been installed throughout the gallery and the adult mummy has been re-housed in a custom-built and environmentally-controlled showcase. Work on the redisplay of the museum's outstanding Egyptology collections will continue during 2010, a generous grant having been made by the DCMS/Wolfson Foundation to support the development of a greatly improved gallery focussed on supporting the museum's extremely active work with schools and families.

But future plans are far more ambitious than this and it is intended that, by 2015, all of the museum's public displays will have been comprehensively reviewed and updated. This represents

a massive undertaking: cases will have to be refurbished and re-lit; galleries reorganised; and collections reinterpreted. It is however a task which is essential if the University is to do full justice to the museum's treasures and to the future generations of museum-goers who will come to Durham to enjoy and learn from them. It is surely an ambition of which Thomas Thacker and Raymond Dawson would have approved.

ABOUT THIS VOLUME
The individual articles in this volume have been penned by a variety of authors and reflect their differing perspectives on the collection. The aim throughout has not been to publish bare descriptions of the museum's treasures, but rather to reflect the many different aspects of the museum's work and the range of people who use and enjoy the collections.

In selecting objects for inclusion we have endeavoured to demonstrate the depth and breadth of our collections. Many of the items chosen will be familiar to regular visitors, but we have sought also to highlight some of the treasures not normally on display to the public. Whilst we hope that there will be much within these covers to delight the reader, we remain conscious that a selection of only 50 objects can never do full justice to the collection and many 'old favourites' have been left out. If this causes disappointment, we can only apologise. We trust however that our readers will understand that the very fact that we have been forced to make such hard choices speaks eloquently for the quality of the treasures which the Oriental Museum is privileged to care for on behalf of Durham University and the world.

Craig Barclay and Rachel Grocke

CHINA

The terms 'China' and 'Chinese' can be used to define a culture, an ancient civilization and – depending on perspective – a modern-day national or multinational entity extending over a large area in East Asia. The People's Republic of China is one of the largest countries in the world, covering more than 9.6 million square kilometres. It is also the world's most populous nation, being home to around one-fifth of the human population. The terrain encompasses mountains, deserts, subtropical forests and rich agricultural land, bounded along the eastern and southern sides by 14,500 kilometres of coastline. The history and culture of this country is equally staggering. Evidence of early agriculture can be dated to around 7000 BCE and, by the Second Millennium BCE, a distinctively Chinese culture which has survived to the present day was already forming under the Shang Dynasty. The most famous achievements of Chinese culture include the invention of paper, gunpowder, the compass and printing.

The Oriental Museum's Chinese collections number more than 10,000 objects. The core of these holdings is formed around two collections: an outstanding group of ceramics acquired from the Rt Hon. Malcolm MacDonald (1901–1981); and a collection built up by Sir Charles Hardinge (1878–1968) which is particularly strong in the areas of jade and other hardstone carvings.

There are around 1,000 pieces of Chinese pottery in the museum's collection, including over 400 items that were originally owned by Malcolm MacDonald. It is truly outstanding in both its typological and chronological breadth, ranging in date and function from Neolithic earthenware storage jars of about 2500 BCE to fine examples of domestic and imperial porcelain of the Qing Dynasty (1644–1911 CE).

The museum's collection of Chinese jade and hardstones consists of almost 2,000 pieces. Jade, which has long been used in China for burial, ritual, decorative and practical uses forms an extensive part of the museum's hardstone collection. In addition to jade, the museum also houses a wide variety of artefacts crafted from other hardstones, which were increasingly widely used by Chinese craftsmen during the Ming (1368–1644 CE) and Qing dynasties. The extraordinary skill of Chinese carvers is amply displayed throughout the museum's collection of work in ivory, bamboo, wood, tortoiseshell and rhinoceros horn.

Painting and calligraphy were traditionally considered to be the highest of art forms in China. The museum boasts examples of each, in various formats, on both silk and paper. Ink rubbings also comprise a notable part of the museum's collection, as do contemporary woodcut prints.

Some of the most spectacular Chinese objects in the museum are the embroidered and woven silks, particularly the official dragon robes and their accessories from the Qing dynasty; whilst notable among the museum's collection of Chinese furniture is a magnificent early 19th-century bed made of *huali* hardwood with carved boxwood and ivory panels. Exceptional examples of laquerware and fine vessels and ornaments in gold, silver and bronze likewise feature prominently in the museum's collection.

The pre-eminence of the Oriental Museum's Chinese collection was formally acknowledged in 2008 when it was awarded *Designated Collection* status in recognition of its national and international importance.

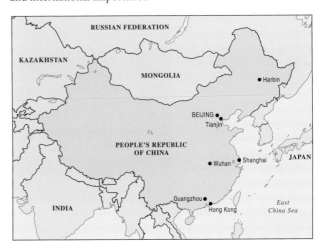

Left: one of the leaves from an album of paintings attributed to the late Ming/early Qing Master, Gong Xian (no. 6).

CHINESE ARCHERY

Crossbow trigger mechanism
Bronze; width 13cm

China
Late Zhou, Qin or Han Dynasty, 399–0 BCE

Gift from Mrs Juliane von Hessert, Henry de Laszlo Collection
DUROM.1992.11

Archers' thumb rings
Jade

China
Varying dates

Gift from Sir Charles Edmund Hardinge
DUROM.1960.995; 1960.3331; 1960.3342

Scholarly opinion varies as to when the crossbow was first used in China, and whilst some writers have argued that weapons of this type may have been in use as early as the second millennium BCE, the earliest surviving bronze trigger mechanism dates to about 600 BCE. What cannot be disputed however is that, from the Warring States period onwards, the crossbow was to become the key weapon in the hands of China's peasant armies.

The most technologically advanced weapon of its day, the crossbow allowed even an unskilled soldier to fire an armour-piercing quarrel with considerable accuracy. Crucial to its success was a complex trigger mechanism which, by the Han Dynasty, had been developed into a piece of precision-cast machinery which was set into the wooden stock of the bow. The bow-string was held in place by a pair of cocking lugs which sat on either side of the bolt. This ensured that the bolt would be released smoothly, as it was able to sit in direct contact with the bow-string. Accuracy was further aided by a trigger which allowed the string to be released without jerking and by the provision of an upright sight which helped the archer to aim his weapon effectively.

According to Zhao Ye's *Romance of Wu and Yue* (circa 40–80 CE), when the King of Yue asked the archer Chen Yin of Chu to explain why the crossbow was so effective, he replied:

'The firing mechanism casing is like the walls of the city: it protects all its "ministers". The trigger-lever is the overlord: all commands originate from it. The release is the enforcer: it controls the officers and men. The latch is the lieutenant: it holds the inner formations in check. The firing mechanism assembly is like the cavalry commander: it commands an advance or a halt. The axle-bolts are passive servants: they comply with whatever is ordered… The point of the quarrel is the killer of hundreds: no-one can dodge it. Birds cannot get away, beasts have no time to flee; for whatever the crossbow is aimed at dies without fail.'

If the crossbow was the weapon of the common soldier, traditional archery was central to the lives of China's social elite. Originally used both for hunting and warfare, the bow and arrow was largely replaced on the battlefield by the crossbow. Archery skills continued to be highly valued however and all gentlemen were expected to be able to handle a bow skillfully, with archery forming an integral part of civil service examinations during the Ming Dynasty.

A key part of the archer's equipment was a ring worn on the thumb. This was used to assist the archer in drawing and releasing the bowstring. Although originally functional objects, archers' rings came in time to be seen as symbols of status and to be worn as a badge of masculinity and rank by rich and educated individuals. Early rings were often made from tough materials such as nephrite jade, horn or ivory, but by the late 1700s more decorative examples were also being carved from colourful jadeite. The form of the rings changed over time, culminating in a fashion for smooth-sided cylinders in the Qing Dynasty. The vast majority of surviving specimens were intended purely for decoration, as the functional rings favoured by serious archers were often made from perishable materials such as bone, leather or horn.

Craig Barclay

Archers' thumb rings.

Terracotta Tang Dynasty Polo Player

2

Ceramic with traces of coloured pigment; height 30cm, length 39cm

China
Tang Dynasty, 800–850 CE

Gift from Rt Hon Malcolm MacDonald
DUROM.1969.35

Many conservators would agree that it is the opportunity to spend many hours in close proximity with a beautifully crafted artefact which motivates them. It was therefore a real treat to work on this Chinese Tang dynasty polo player. The female polo player riding a horse is depicted in low-fired terracotta, traces of pigment hinting at the colourful finish it would once have had. As well as being a lovely object to conserve, it was also to prove to be quite a challenge.

A break around the female rider's waist revealed the cavity within the clay – the object is hollow to lessen its density and reduce the risk of cracking during firing. Reattaching these thin walls therefore presented a problem: simply to stick the two halves together was very unlikely to survive the test of time as the join would be weak. One would not choose to use a strong adhesive, for if the piece were to break again it would be the modern repair one would want to fail, rather than another, weaker area in the original clay. Traces of old repairs were evident around the break showing that, unsurprisingly, this was not the first time an accident had happened in the horse's 1,000-year history.

The difficulty of rejoining the pieces was exacerbated by one of the features which gives it its vitality – the sense of movement is captured by the acute angle at which the rider sits, clearly at full tilt ready to smack an imaginary ball. The balance of the piece was therefore precarious, and the join would need to be strong enough to support the weight of this extended body.

A common practice in sculpture conservation is to insert a rigid dowel when fixing a break to impart internal support to the weakened break area; could this technique be employed here? As the object was hollow, to do so would involve finding a way to plug the cavity in horse and rider to hold the dowel. Moreover to meet today's conservation standards, the whole construction needed to be reversible.

After much deliberation I took a cast from both cavities using dental silicon rubber (tools designed for dentists are often invaluable to conservators!). With these it was possible to make moulds from which plaster of paris casts could be created. Adhering the casts within the cavities using a weak, reversible adhesive, the voids were effectively plugged with a soft material compatible with the terracotta. A hole was then drilled into each to receive the dowel. So that the aluminium dowel could easily be removed in future, a polished sleeve was fixed into the plug in the polo player's body which the dowel attached into the horse's back could slide in and out of. Much time was spent getting the angle of the dowel right so that the polo player sat at the correct angle. With a little soluble adhesive applied to the break edges and the tops of the plugs, horse and rider were thus reunited. As there had been a small loss of material around the break, a little toned fill was applied to this area so that it would not distract the viewer.

A fine new stand was made by a mount maker to hold the polo player securely and horse and rider were ready to go back on display. One would hope they can now remain arrested in the moment of play for many years to come.

Diana de Bellaigue

The polo player and horse before conservation.

Song Dynasty Bowl with Mandarin Duck Design

3

Porcelain with incised decoration, creamy white glaze and copper rim-band; diameter 23.4cm, height 6.2cm

China, Hebei Province (Ding kilns)
Northern Song Dynasty, 960–1127 CE

Gift from the Rt Hon Malcolm MacDonald
DUROM.1969.40

The Chinese ceramic industry experienced a period of considerable growth and innovation under the Song Dynasties. While their predecessors, the Tang, are characterised as colourful and cosmopolitan, Song culture was built on a large-scale central administration with a strong respect for classical Confucian tradition. The art of the Song period is characterised by an intellectual, didactic approach. In ceramics this led to a pursuit of the perfect harmony between a monochrome glaze and the shape of the vessel. Words often used to describe Song ceramics include serene, pure and subtle. In Chinese literature Song wares have been described as 'resembling jade, silver, snow or ice.'

Economic expansion under this regime included a considerable increase in overseas trade from China's great sea ports. Chinese silk and ceramics were traded across Southeast Asia and to the Near East in return for luxuries such as spices, ivory, pearls, amber and rhinoceros horn. To exploit these new markets to the full, Song potters increased output, reduced costs and enhanced the quality of their ceramics.

One of the Song Dynasty innovations was a move to coal rather than wood firing in large-scale kilns. This reduced costs and increased output – a revolutionary step not taken in Europe for another 1000 years. One of the by-products of using coal rather than wood is the creation of an oxidizing atmosphere which results in the characteristic warm, ivory colour of the glaze seen on this dish.

Another major innovation of the period was *fushao* ('upside-down fringe') firing. This method involved stacking wares upside-down in the kiln, resting on top of one another on special props. This meant that four to five times as many objects could be fired at once – greatly improving efficiency. It also resulted in a characteristic unglazed rim, covered here with a band of copper.

The decoration on this bowl shows the popular Song motif of two mandarin ducks. Ducks were already a popular motif in Tang art, partly it seems due to Indian influences. They are however rarely seen as a design on ceramics produced before the Song Dynasty. A pair of mandarin ducks is one of the most frequent symbols of happy marriage in China. They were chosen because these ducks were considered to mate for life and if one of them should die the other would pine away. A bowl such as this would have made an ideal wedding gift.

This exceptionally fine piece was originally acquired by Malcolm MacDonald, whose collection of ceramics first came to Durham University as a loan in 1956. Happily, the museum was able to acquire the collection in 1969 and it continues to form one of the cornerstones of the Chinese collections. Of all the pieces he gifted to Durham this Song Dynasty bowl was MacDonald's personal favourite. It was one of the most expensive pieces he ever purchased, but in the introduction to the museum's catalogue of his collection he writes:

'*…this was one of those incidents which taught me the invaluable lesson that occasionally (though not too often!) the wisest way to spend money is on some object of irresistible beauty which is so commercially valuable that you cannot possibly afford to buy it, but also so aesthetically priceless that you cannot afford not to buy it. If you fail to get it, its ghost haunts you for ever afterwards… if I owned no other piece of Chinese porcelain, I should still be a proud and satisfied collector.*'

Rachel Grocke

SHU FU PORCELAIN CUP WITH DRAGON DESIGN

4

Porcelain with white glaze; diameter 13.7cm, height 12.4cm

China, Jiangxi province, Jingdezhen
Yuan Dynasty, 1279–1368 CE

Gift from Rt Hon Malcolm MacDonald
DUROM.1969.141

Museums rarely display ceramics in a way that appeals to a potter. Pots lined up neatly next to each other in showcases fail to answer the basic questions which a potter may have – how has this pot been made and how successful is its execution? Pots are the product as much of the hands as the eye. Information gleaned through fingertips is just as important as that coming through the retina, and so the potter's questions can only satisfactorily be answered by handling the object itself. Many pots such as bowls will have decoration both on the inside as well as the outside and in a display there will be an opportunity to admire the decoration on one surface, with perhaps only a tantalising glimpse of the decoration on the other. With dishes and plates this dichotomy is even more acute – display a dish vertically on a stand to reveal the main decoration and the underside is totally obscured.

Another dilemma for the potter is the emphasis in museum displays on only the best of wares. 'Museum' or 'exhibition' quality describing an item in a collection condemns the less than perfect, removing from general view any object that does not meet this exacting standard set not by the viewing public but by the museum curator. But in all production there is a range of quality, and to be able to see pots that are less well executed only serves to highlight the achievement of those that are truly successful. Emphasis on museum quality exerts a subtle and insidious metamorphosis on the pot, turning it from the functional and utilitarian ware that it started life as into a cold and inanimate object in a glass case.

The delicate stem cup form produced at Jingdezhen, the acknowledged centre of the Chinese porcelain industry, was a new shape derived from the Mongolian taste of the then rulers of China, and became established in the potter's repertoire of later periods. Intended as a wine cup, it originated as wine making developed in China. Porcelain ware production was industrialised and different workers were responsible for separate processes – a far cry from the studio potter who sees through the pot from beginning to end. The stem cup was thrown on the wheel, the stem created separately from the bowl. While the clay was still sufficiently workable, the bowl was pressed onto a mould carved with the design of the five-clawed dragon pursuing a flaming pearl, then carefully pared down to thin the wall of the bowl sufficiently to ensure translucency. Porcelain is a very unforgiving medium to throw on the wheel and paring the clay when leather hard is the only practical way to achieve a thin-walled vessel.

The stem, by comparison, is much less worked and relatively thick. The two are joined by a coil of clay, part of which is clearly visible in the inside of the stem at the join. The glaze would most likely be applied to the unfired pot – requiring skill from long experience to avoid the pot collapsing when wet – and then the cup was fired. It is remarkable that the Chinese potters were able to fire successfully without technical aids, relying on the eye to determine the appropriate heat in the kiln. Surviving evidence suggests that many firings were a disaster, with the whole load of wares spoiled in the process. It is thus all the more remarkable that pots such as the Durham stem cup survive.

The stem cup has also had a life as a used vessel, subject to wear, tear, and breakage, but nevertheless remains intact. The journey from the Jingdezhen pottery, where craftsmen developed techniques to combine the elements of earth, water, fire and air, has lasted several centuries, bringing to us this object of enduring beauty still to be admired today.

John Hall

RHINOCEROS HORN LIBATION CUP

Rhinoceros horn; height 11.5cm, width 14.5cm

China
Late Ming or Early Qing Dynasty, 17th century CE

Gift from Mrs Juliane von Hessert, Henry de Laszlo collection
DUROM.1992.140

Fossil remains suggest that at one time rhino roamed over the whole area which now forms the People's Republic of China. Written sources however suggest that by the Song Dynasty rhino were already rare and that by the Yuan Dynasty they were extinct within China's borders. Rhino are naturally timid and retreat from areas of human occupation, while at the same time their horned and armoured appearance engenders fear, making them a target for human hunters. It is perhaps both the rarity of rhino and the danger and difficulty involved in hunting them that led to rhino horn becoming so highly prized among the Chinese.

From earliest times rhino horn appears to have been linked to the wish for long life and even immortality. The *Book of Songs*, said to have been first written down around 500 BCE by Confucius himself, contains a reference to raising the rhinoceros horn up 'with wishes for a long life'. The First Emperor, Qin Shihuang, famous for his desire for immortality, is reputed to have sent an army of 5000 men to open up trade routes to the south east, in order to acquire rhino horn and elephant tusks. By the 4th century CE rhino horn cups were said to have the ability to prevent death in a more direct way: poisoned wine placed in such a cup was said to bubble or foam, revealing the presence of the toxin. Tales of this fabulous animal – whose single magical horn could prevent death by poisoning and perhaps even confer immortality – spread to Europe along trade routes. It seems likely that such tales are the origin of our unicorn myth.

The carving of rhinoceros horn was a complex process. First the horn had to be prepared. The rough outer layer and base of the horn were removed, and the carver would then coat the chosen section of horn with oil, lanolin, clear lacquer or natural glue to prevent splitting or shrinkage. Next the carver would sketch the chosen design onto the horn in black ink. Chinese carvers became skilled in creating carvings that used as much as possible of the precious horn by producing designs that followed the shape of each individual horn. Carving would be carried out with chisels and gouges and once the design had been achieved it would then be polished to smooth out the tool-marks. Sometimes pieces were also dyed with natural dyes such as walnut, sepia or squid ink. Finally the piece would be polished to a high gloss. As well as ceremonial cups, such as the one shown here, figure and animal carvings, snuff bottles and other objects were also created from rhino horn.

This cup shows a Chinese scholar standing on a bridge above a waterfall. To his right stands a servant holding a musical instrument. Scholars commanded great respect in China from the time of Confucius onwards. The system of Imperial examinations introduced in the Han Dynasty (221 BCE–212 CE) demanded high levels of study and the hardworking scholar was seen as a symbol of self-discipline and diligence. Behind the scholar a long, coiling pine tree forms the handle of the cup and comes up over the rim. Pine trees, together with cedars, ranked above all other trees in the symbolism of Chinese art. Like the scholar, they also represented the quality of self-discipline.

Rachel Grocke

Eight Album Leaves Attributed to Gong Xian (1618–1689)

Ink and slight colour on paper; height 34cm, width 35cm

China
Qing Dynasty, 1644–1689 CE

Gift from Dr HN Spalding
DUROM.GQ13

This series of eight ink on paper album leaves, three of which are shown here, is attributed to the late Ming – early Qing master Gong Xian 龔賢 (1618–1689 CE). They are part of the museum's foundation collection and were a gift from HN Spalding, a generous benefactor who also funded lectureships in Chinese and Indian studies at Durham. There is no prior provenance, but the turmoil in China in the 1930s and 1940s resulted in many family treasures finding their way on to the market as people struggled to survive.

Authenticity is a major problem in Chinese painting. Westerners tend to take a rather rigid view but Chinese have traditionally been more relaxed, seeing copying as an indicator of esteem not fraud. This has made authentication difficult, and the 'attributed to Gong Xian' reflects this. The signature on one of the album leaves is typical of Gong Xian, and there is also a seal bearing one of Gong Xian's *hao* names, Chaizhang 柴丈 (Old Man Woodcutter). The subject matter and painting techniques are also characteristic of Gong Xian, although on a smaller scale than his renowned large hanging scrolls. The scenery is typical of his Jiangnan region, with craggy mountains and verdant valleys, while the brushwork, using *tu bi* 秃筆 (bald brush), *jian bi* 尖筆 (sharp brush), and *ji mo* 積墨 (accumulated ink) techniques are features of his style. Album leaves had been popular since the Song dynasty but, as William Watson observed,

'the second half of the seventeen century saw a climax in album painting in the classical landscape style'. This format has resulted in a crease down the centre of each leaf where it has been folded, yet it has also helped to retain the colour, which, although delicate and subtle, remains fresh.

The subject matter of these album leaves is taken to be the four seasons plus four transitions, a popular topic reflecting the change and impermanence that exist in human life as much as in nature. This is intended both as a reminder and a comfort. Gong Xian's life was greatly affected by the cataclysmic changes resulting from the fall of the Ming dynasty. His hopes for a comfortable life as a scholar official were dashed and although he is regarded as part of the *wenren* 'literati' painting tradition, he was forced to 'abase' himself and become a professional painter. Landscape painting and calligraphy were the ultimate expressions of art in traditional China. The ideal for the scholar was to commune with nature, walking among the mountains and streams, but this was generally not practicable for a busy official, so taking out a landscape painting and allowing the mind to wander its paths was a substitute for this. Traditional Chinese scholars were characterised as 'Confucians in office and Daoists out of office', an apt description of Gong Xian.

Don Starr

Boulder Carved in the Form of a Mountain Landscape

7

Nephrite jade; height 16cm

China
Qing Dynasty, 18th century CE

Gift from Sir Charles Edmund Hardinge
DUROM.1960.2205

It is tempting to think that a series of advertisements placed in *The Times* newspaper during November and December 1934 might have initiated Sir Charles Hardinge's purchase of this jade carving. Edith Lee was an obscure antiques dealer whose shop was situated at 28 Charlotte Street, off Tottenham Court Road in London and Sir Charles paid just £15 for it. Edith Lee promoted her old English furniture, watercolours, Chinese porcelain, pottery and jades, as 'charming, cheap Christmas gifts' and she formed one of a small group of out-of-the-way London dealers who, according to Sir Charles, rarely knew the value of their stock. On average, he seldom paid more than £20 each for his jades.

Sir Charles Edmund Hardinge (1878–1968), fifth Baronet, had family associations with Stanhope in Weardale, County Durham. He began collecting jade in 1917, when recuperating from an illness. Walking with the aid of crutches he frequented 'junk shops', as he called them, as places where he could rest. Even as a small boy, Sir Charles had collected, concentrating primarily on small animal figures. Now he began to be fascinated by one material in particular, jade. Because of his training as a petrologist he became concerned with the different types of stone that were described as jade and set about defining them into their more precise geological family names of amphibole and pyroxene. His findings were published in 1961 as *Jade: Fact and Fable*. From 1921 until 1959, Sir Charles kept detailed records of his purchases, itemising date of acquisition, a short description of the material,

price paid, from whom purchased and, if relevant, when it was sold, gifted or exchanged and for how much. At the time the collection was donated to the Oriental Museum, Sir Charles had collected over 2,500 jades and other hardstones, many of them of the highest quality.

This carving of a mountain, peopled with the three star gods of longevity, prosperity and happiness being worshipped by Daoist pilgrims, can be compared with traditional Chinese landscape painting, albeit in three dimensions. Such carvings became fashionable after the latter half of the 18th century during the reign of the Qianlong Emperor (1736–1795), when, following the annexation of the regions around Khotan and Yarkand in Central Asia, more plentiful supplies of nephrite were available. This piece takes its inspiration from the massive boulders carved by the imperial workshops, the largest of which, measuring 224 cm in height and weighing seven tons, was finished in 1788 and depicted the legendary Chinese ruler Yu the Great pacifying the flood. For the Chinese, mountains were seen as spiritual places – an intermediary realm between heaven and earth – and the use of jade would have emphasised the physical relationship of the stone with that which it represents, as would its hardness (and therefore indestructibility), which was symbolic of immortality. The mountain carving can therefore be seen to embody the physical, spiritual and cosmological.

Nick Pearce

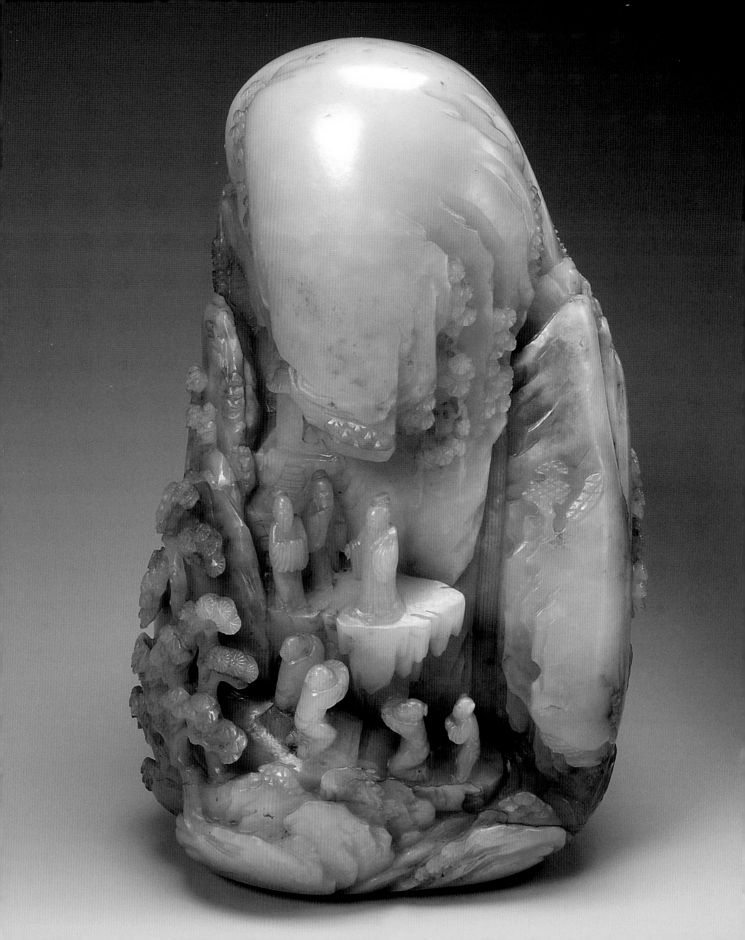

ASTRONOMICAL CLOCK

8

Wood, metal and glass; height 62cm, width 38cm

China, probably manufactured in the Canton area
Qing Dynasty, 18th century CE

Gift from Sir Charles Edmund Hardinge
DUROM.1960.880

This remarkable astronomical clock, on the face of which is engraved an intriguing star chart, is one of only two known exemplars worldwide. Its counterpart, in the Forbidden City at Beijing, differs from it only in minor details.

Although the Durham clock bears no maker's name, it was probably made in Canton (present day Guangzhou). The movement is Chinese, but it is based on an English design of around 1790 CE. The Beijing version is known to have been made at Suzhou around 1880 and was presented to the Chinese emperor. Both Canton and Suzhou were clock-making centres, but why the Suzhou artefact so closely resembles that produced almost a century earlier in Canton remains a mystery.

The Durham clock's attractive carved wooden stand is typical of that found in a middle-class household in China during the 18th century. At the edge of the clock face are two brass rings: a fixed outer ring and an inner ring which revolves with the main dial. The outer ring is marked with the 12 *shi* or 'double-hours', which make up a full day and night. Each *shi* is divided into two equal parts: *chu* ('initial half') and *zheng* ('central half'). Noon (the middle of the double-hour *wu*) is at the top; this is identified by a small round marker.

Both pointers move in the usual (clockwise) direction. The hour hand makes a full sweep of the dial every 24 hours. The slightly longer minute hand makes a full circuit every (single) hour. Whereas the outer edge of the fixed brass ring is divided into 60 *fen* ('minutes'), the inner edge is subdivided into 96 *ke* ('quarters': of an hour). Hence the clock can be used for telling the time in both Western and Chinese cultures.

The inner brass ring marks the seasons. Each day this ring – together with the main dial – turns clockwise through one degree, thus making a full revolution in a year. The ring is engraved with the names of the *qi* ('solar terms': 24 equal divisions of the year). Both edges of the ring are further subdivided into 360 *du* ('degrees').

On the main face of the clock is a chart showing the brighter stars visible from Southern China. On the chart, the most prominent feature is the Milky Way (*Tianhe* – the 'Celestial River') but in all around 850 stars are represented by small red circles. These stars are joined into about 160 groups, representing the most significant of the traditional Chinese constellations, including the 28 *xiu* ('lunar lodges'). With few exceptions, the Chinese constellations differ widely – both in shape and size – from the star groupings adopted in Western culture.

Although virtually all Chinese planar star maps depict the night sky as seen from the Earth's surface, the chart on the Durham clock face instead represents the constellations in reverse – as depicted on a celestial globe. A possible explanation for choosing this convention might be to permit clockwise revolution of the dial. Measurements on the star chart reveal that the positions of the brightest stars are fairly accurately marked: typically to within about 1 degree. However, the locations of many of the fainter stars are only approximately charted and hence the constellation shapes are, in general, somewhat inaccurate.

At the edge of the star chart – just beyond the constellation figures – is a circle divided into twelve equal sections, each extending over an arc of 30 degrees. These divisions represent the twelve *ci* ('Jupiter stations'), which were important in Chinese astrology. Each of these stations was associated with one of the twelve states into which ancient China was divided. Although the *ci* have some parallels with the signs of the Western zodiac, there are fundamental differences between the two systems.

F Richard Stephenson

9

HAND-EMBROIDERED LOTUS SHOES

Silk; length 9cm, width 3.8cm, height 6cm

China
Qing Dynasty, 1644–1912 CE

Gift from Mrs GF Dixon
DUROM.1974.5

Few people doubt the ability of museum objects to teach people about the past: they have an almost unique potential to inspire development of knowledge and an understanding of different cultures. Indeed, it was the recognition and embracing of this potential that led to the establishment of the Oriental Museum in 1960, and education in its widest sense remains at the heart of the work undertaken today. In addition to being a home for scholarly research, the Oriental Museum welcomes children and young people to use and learn from its collections and it is clear that the 'treasures' of the museum speak very powerfully to this age group.

An excellent example of how our treasures can be used to inspire children and young people is provided by these beautiful silk lotus shoes from the late Qing dynasty. By asking very simple questions such as 'What are these?'; 'What are they made from?'; 'What colours and patterns can you see?'; 'Who would have worn them?'; and 'Why would they have worn them?', the children learn about the practice of foot binding, the stories and myths about its origins, cultural practices associated with the process and the importance of symbolism in Chinese culture.

Recounting the stories about the origins of foot binding immediately engages the attention of children. In one Cinderella-style story, dating from the Tang dynasty, an orphan called Yexian dropped a slipper fleeing from a Cave Festival celebration. The slipper was sold to the Tuohan king who searched long and hard for its owner before finding Yexian and marrying her. In another version, Yao-niang, a consort of the emperor Li Yu bound her feet before she danced so that they resembled new moons. So impressed were the other consorts by Yao-niang's graceful walk that they too started to bind their feet. A third story has the women in the Chinese court binding their feet out of sympathy for an empress who had club feet.

What generates the most discussion and debate, however, is their size. Children are intrigued by the smallness of the shoes and are eager to learn more about the actual practice of foot binding. Although often shocked by the fact that the process started when girls were aged between five and eight, our children are, perhaps, more surprised by the fact that the women embraced the custom and made it an essential part of their culture. The women's pride in having small feet is reflected in the exquisite embroidery on the slippers. Embroidered on red silk, suggesting that these shoes were intended for a wedding, the principal motifs on this pair are flowers and birds. Other common emblems were butterflies, dragons, bats and fish. The challenge of working out the symbolism deployed on these slippers and other Chinese objects in the Museum is one of the most favourably received activities undertaken by visiting groups.

The thrill of seeing real objects undoubtedly leaves a lasting impression on young visitors to the Museum, bringing subjects to life in a way that cannot be achieved as easily in a classroom. It seems apt therefore to conclude with the remarks of an eight-year-old who, when asked what they had most enjoyed about their visit replied: 'Handling artefacts, reacting, mostly everything about this brilliant day out.'

Sarah Price

EMBROIDERED DRAGON ROBE

Textile; length (nape-hem) 129cm, width (cuff-cuff) 216cm

China
Qing Dynasty, 1644–1912 CE

Purchased
DUROM.1966.56

Bright and flamboyant Dragon Robes – inextricably associated with Imperial China – reinforce a European expectation that things Oriental should also be exotic. With their magnificent colours and detailed embroidery, they are hugely popular with a wide spectrum of museum visitors. Like all textiles however, they are fragile. The care, conservation and storage of such objects require specific knowledge, skills and a deep understanding of textiles. Such expertise is hard to come by and is usually acquired over a long period of time through study, perseverance and practical experience.

When, in the 1990s, the university decided to install a new *Marvels of China* gallery at the Oriental Museum, the curatorial staff discovered that many of the items in the textile collection would need to be given conservation treatment prior to being put on display. At around the same time, members of the Durham branch of the Embroiderers' Guild were taking an increasing interest in textile conservation. A 'marriage made in heaven' was in the offing.

A professional conservator was invited to speak to members of the Guild and subsequently organised a training session, using the museum's collection. Thus was the link made between curatorial staff and enthusiastic embroiderer volunteers. Members of the embroiderers' group brought a wealth of accumulated textile knowledge and needle skills to the task. The new gallery proved to be a great success, and a core group of volunteers has continued to aid the museum in work with textiles, receiving further specialist training from time to time as required.

Collections-based work is invariably carried out in a disciplined and systematic manner. Preliminary assessment includes writing a full description; identifying constituent materials and construction methods; highlighting surface embellishment; and identifying areas of damage. Suggestions for possible cleaning, conservation and storage are considered, and an individual action plan is prepared in collaboration with members of the museum's curatorial team.

Initially, most articles require a gentle clean with specialist vacuuming equipment. With the aim of minimal intervention, work to stabilise the artefact is then carried out. This can involve minimal stitching to hold down embellishments or applying fine net to the surface to support the fabric and prevent further deterioration. A suitable position for attaching an identification label is identified, and appropriate storage materials are prepared. Depending upon the nature of the textile, these may take the form of a box, a roll or a hanger. All are constructed individually to fit the object.

One of the garments upon which the embroiderers have worked recently is a fine Dragon Robe. The wearing of a five-clawed dragon symbol on clothing was restricted to members of the imperial court. The dragons on this robe have been worked in the technique of couching. Thin strips of beaten gold wrapped around a silk core create a gold thread which is laid down on the base fabric in intricate patterns and secured in place with tiny stitches of silk thread. Additional details such as the eyes, claws and spine are then added in satin-stitch. Many of the other symbols on the robe, such as the peonies and fish, are worked in Peking knots.

The Dragon Robe illustrated is in an overall good condition apart from the cuffs and border at the neck and front. Here, the base fabric of black silk has been attacked by light and has deteriorated, leaving the embroidery with little support. These areas have been netted to provide the necessary support. For the embroiderers, their involvement in this type of work is a two-way process. The volunteers are able to examine textiles at close quarters, learning about construction methods, design and colour. These provide inspiration for creative interpretations, which may then be exhibited alongside the source artefacts. In turn, the museum is able to conserve more than would otherwise be possible.

Embroiderers' Guild Volunteers

EXPORT PAINTINGS ON PITH

Pith with water colour painting; page height 21cm, width 34cm

China, Guangzhou (Canton)
Qing Dynasty, 19th century CE

Gift from Miss MO Horne
DUROM.1968.128

In his book, translated from the French in 1812 as *China: its Costume, Arts, Manufactures, &c*, M. Breton exclaims that:

> *'The annual importation of tea into England is prodigious. A century ago it did not amount to fifty pounds weight a year; in 1777 it was six millions; and in 1795, nearly twenty-eight millions.'*

Over that period and up to the Treaty of Nanking, 1842, Canton was the only Chinese port officially open to foreign trade. The influx of Western visitors increased in proportion to the trade in tea and these visitors demanded pictorial souvenirs of this distant and exotic land.

Chinese painted export wallpapers had been in vogue in the great English and French houses since the mid-18th century. Spolium and his followers in Canton had painted large-scale portraits, landscapes and ship-paintings in a style acceptable to affluent Westerners from about 1770. By the early years of the 19th century there was however a much wider demand for less expensive pictures for individual travellers to take home. The painters in Canton responded by adopting a new exotic material, developing a style to suit the new surface and producing small pictures, often bound into albums, on a very wide range of subjects.

This new material was pith, cut into sheets directly from the inner spongy tissue of the stem of the small tree *Tetrapanax Papyrifera*, native to south-west China and the highlands of Taiwan. Pith was already well known to the Chinese for many uses including stuffing pillows and cushions, packing, lining coffins, in Chinese medicine and for craft work and toys for children. Since the early years of the Chinese empire small sheets of pith (7.5cm x 7.5cm) had been cut to make flowers for courtiers to wear in their hair. Nevertheless, pith does not seem to have been used for painting before about 1820. Cutting larger sheets for painting was so skilled that it took three years to learn and one sheet would sell at the same price, 1½d, as 100 of the smaller size. At the time the price of tea to the East India Company in Canton was between 8d and 3/- per pound.

Pith is cut directly from the plant, dried and trimmed but not processed or coated in any way. Though often referred to as 'rice-paper' it is neither a manufactured paper, nor has it anything to do with rice. The cut surface is cellular and throws off the light more like a miniature mosaic than smooth paper. The opaque watercolour used by the painters sits on the surface and allows great detail since it does not bleed off. The natural sheen of the pith, enhanced by the artists' skilful use of gouache, made these little paintings very popular as souvenirs and in the 1830s there were said to be 30 studios or shops on the river-bank outside the city of Canton where they were made and sold.

Henry Sirr, Vice-Consul of Hong Kong, describes in his book on China a visit in about 1847 to the studio of Lam Qua where he saw 'some complete gems, being water-colour drawings upon what is usually termed rice-paper'. Among the most intriguing was a set corresponding to Shakespeare's *Seven Ages of Man*. Nine pictures from just such a set (artist unknown) are among the most remarkable of the paintings in the Oriental Museum collection.

Ifan Williams

Right: Kow-towing in absolute acceptance of the authority of the examiner.
Overleaf: New-born baby with nurse.

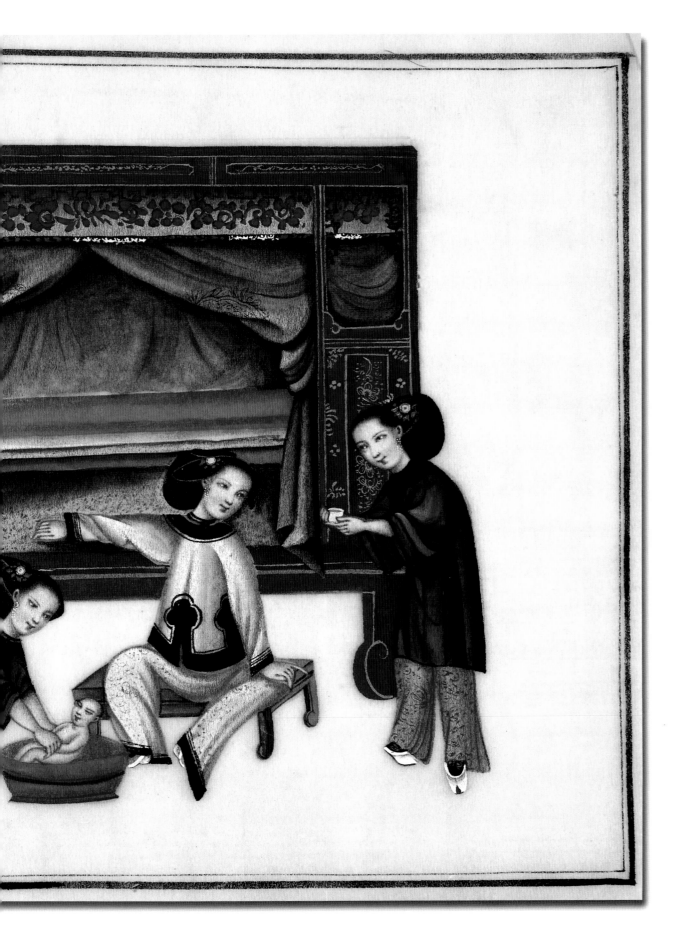

34/100   秋的風采   兆梅 Chao Mei 1998

12

CHAO MEI AND HIS AUTUMN GLORY

Paper; page height 82.9cm, width 69cm

China, Heilongjiang, Beidahuang School, made by Chao Mei
1998 CE

Purchased
DUROM.2009.13

The long tradition of printmaking in China dates back over a millennium. Highly sophisticated woodblock prints of religious images were already being produced during the Tang period (618–907 CE), whilst the printing of books and illustrations reached a peak during the Ming Dynasty (1368–1644). In modern China, printmaking as a creative medium was promoted by the writer Lu Xun (1881–1936), who introduced Western printmaking to young Chinese artists during the 1930s. Since then woodblock printmaking has been a primary medium for Chinese printmaking artists.

During the early 1960s woodblock prints created by a group of young amateur printmaking artists from the Beidahuang region had a strong impact on the art field which has lasted until today. Their colourful and powerful prints depicted scenes of the cultivation of China's wasteland. Known as the Great Northern Wildness School, the printmakers were agricultural workers: former liberation army soldiers who had been sent to the region to cultivate the 'wasteland'. A pioneering representative of the School was Chao Mei (晁楣 b. 1931, Heze, Shandong). Chao's most notable contributions to the technique of printmaking were his breakthroughs in multi-colour non-key woodblock printing techniques, which enabled the depictions of complicated colour variations.

Chao's works are mostly in dense and rich colours which reflect his deep attachment to the northern land. Prior to the late 1970s, Chao's work was primarily realist – depicting agricultural workers and harvest scenes – and reflected the Soviet socialist realism style which dominated Chinese art. Following the open door policy in 1979, Chinese artists partially regained their freedom of expression and Chao's work gradually came to focus on expressing his feelings and pure natural or romantic beauty; the political messages of his work gradually being replaced by a poetic atmosphere. Since the 1990s, his work has shown greater simplicity in form and boldness and freedom in expression.

Autumn Glory demonstrates the artist's later style. It was produced for a portfolio of 60 Chinese printmaking artists' work which was assembled by the Muban Foundation in London. This work depicts an autumn scene in north-east China, which is famed for its fertile black earth and dense forests. It was printed from five separate woodblocks which were cut on five-layer birch wood and printed with oil-based offset inks. The vivid bright yellow birch trees standing dramatically against an almost black background creates an illusion of sound and movement which gives one an impression of a breeze blowing over the yellow trees. This work can be regarded as a celebration of autumn, of nature and as a reflection of the artist's robust, solid and passionate soul. Chao's work in some ways reflects the degree to which Chinese artists have both adopted and rejected Western conventions.

He Weimin

CHINA: TIBETAN AUTONOMOUS REGION

In geographical terms the Tibetan plateau is a vast region in Central Asia, occupying an area of around 2.5 million square kilometres at an average elevation of almost 5,000 metres above sea level. This 'roof of the world' lies at the crossroads between China and the Indian Subcontinent and is dominated by the Tibetan Autonomous Region of the People's Republic of China.

The Oriental Museum's Tibetan collection is heavily focussed on Buddhist religious material. Buddhism was introduced into the area in the 7th or 8th century CE, from where it spread into Mongolia and other central Asian areas. Particular features of Tibetan Buddhism include the special status of the teacher or 'Lama', a particular focus on the relationship between life and death and an emphasis on the use of ritual, mantras and meditation.

Elements of earlier Tibetan faiths, including the presence of some gods and spirits, have been incorporated into Tibetan Buddhism. These appear alongside buddhas and *bodhisattvas* in the rich visual art tradition that has also developed within this strand of Buddhism. The use of pictures, architecture, prayer wheels and flags provide abundant reminders of the presence of the spiritual domain in the physical world.

The Oriental Museum's collection includes an outstanding collection of *thangkas*. These painted or embroidered hangings are used in both temples and domestic settings as a teaching tool, source of visual and mental inspiration, particularly for meditation, and also in ritual contexts. The collection also includes other ritual implements, weapons, seals, furniture, musical instruments, prayer wheels, talismans in various materials, textiles, cloisonné, reliquaries, ritual and domestic vessels in various materials, and woodblock prints.

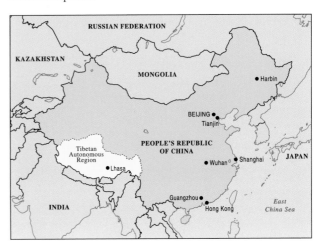

Left: Human skull-cup (no. 14).

THANGKA SHOWING THE
GODDESS GREEN TARA

13

Silk; height 72.5cm, width 68.2cm

China, Tibet
Qing Dynasty, 1750–1899 CE

Gift from the Marquess of Zetland
DUROM.2000.18

This *thangka*, or religious banner, showing the goddess Green Tara, is unusual because it has been embroidered rather than painted. Sometimes called 'scroll paintings', *thangkas* are composite objects. The image is produced on cotton or silk fabric and mounted on a textile frame, often brocade, set between wooden dowels so that it can be easily rolled up and carried. A fine silk cover is unfurled to protect the picture from dust or from the smoking butter lamps found in Tibetan monasteries.

Thangkas are empowering objects. Commissioning one is thought to bring merit. They are produced to mark important life events, to aid good rebirth and to tell tales of the Buddha and *bodhisattvas*. They are sometimes used in public processions, and may be carried by teachers to illustrate their tales. They can also be used privately, during meditation, to bolster or clarify visualizations.

This *thangka* depicts the goddess Green Tara, who is thought to grant protection and help to deal with everyday dangers. According to some sources, worshipping Green Tara can deliver one from the 'eight great perils', which are generally taken to be fire, water, lions, elephants, imprisonment, snakes, thieves and disease caused by evil spirits.

Queen Mary may well have viewed this particular *thangka* in the 1930s. It was owned by the second Marquess of Zetland at the time, Lawrence John Lumley Dundas (1876–1961), whose estate was at Aske, near Richmond in North Yorkshire. The Queen, accompanied by the Princess Royal and the Earl of Harewood, visited for the day in September 1937 and *The Times* reported that, 'The party took luncheon at Aske Hall and then Queen Mary spent some time inspecting the art treasures and the grounds and gardens.'

The Marquess of Zetland had gathered his art treasures during a lifetime of travel in Asia. He served as Governor of Bengal from 1917–1922, and, following his return to Britain, as Secretary of State for India from 1935–1940. He was widely respected in India for his accessible, respectful and calm approach to administration. As the *Dictionary of National Biography* records, the Marquess 'devoted his life to finding a means of blending Indian culture and aspirations with the continuance of what he saw as the benefits of British rule'. He wrote many books about his travels, he studied Buddhism closely, and he was fascinated by Asian philosophy and culture.

Frances Larson

14

HUMAN SKULL-CUP

Bone, metal, stone; height 22cm including lid, width 15cm

China, Tibet
Qing Dynasty, 19th century CE

Purchased
DUROM.1962.226

The Tibetan skull-cup (*kapala*) held by the Oriental Museum is a beautiful example of an artistic and ritual item dating from the 19th century CE. Created using a human skull divided into cup and lid ornately decorated with gems, the skull-cup is considered an inheritance of ancient sacrificial rituals and can often be seen held in the left hand of Tibetan deities such as Dharmapalas. In Tibetan monasteries its use is as a ritual bowl or libation vessel holding wine in place of blood and even bread or dough cakes (*torma*) made to resemble human eyes, ears and tongues in place of flesh.

Whilst the use of human remains to create a decorative or even ritual item is a concept far removed from modern western practice, there are many religions and cultures which view human remains and death itself very differently. Perhaps the best example of this can be found in Mexico where The Day of The Dead, also called All Souls Day, is an annual event and public holiday in November, aimed at remembering and celebrating those who have passed away. Thus, whilst in Britain death is rarely celebrated and often feared, in Mexico and other parts of the world it is viewed as an integral part of existence. The society we live in is highly disconnected, by choice, from discussing death.

> *'The human body is a paradox. Objectively, it is a thing like any other thing. Subjectively, it is part of ourselves. Like someone in a coma, a dead body has left the world of social interaction and perception, but not the world of social relationships.'*
> GUIDELINES ON POLICY FOR HUMAN REMAINS IN SURREY MUSEUMS.

It is because of the many different attitudes people have to death and dying that the display of human remains is a contentious issue in museums. A museum must make decisions true to its fundamental ethos – that of promoting learning – whilst presenting human remains sensitively and only where necessary in order to enhance visitor understanding of a given subject. It must not be forgotten that human remains from archaeological sites and other contexts are direct evidence of past human experience and can serve to educate and foster greater understanding of how societies have evolved from the very earliest prehistoric periods until the present, perhaps even offering an insight into the future.

Viewed within the walls of a museum the skull-cup – although created from human remains – can nevertheless perhaps be considered within a different social context. Often the remains used to make ritual items were left by high lamas to their monastery for that very purpose. Due to the transformation of the bones into what might be considered an 'object' or 'artefact', the observer can perhaps disconnect from its parts and focus on the whole. In doing so however, does the 'object' lose something of its meaning and thus its very purpose?

If this was where the learning experience stopped, then it could be argued that it does. However, an artefact of this nature – one that serves as a reminder of the transient nature of existence – cannot fail to inspire the observer to delve more into its reasons for being, its creation and its purpose. For this to happen, the observer must consider the use of human remains in its creation. This in turn compels the observer to question their own beliefs and feelings about death. If all this can be achieved through the display of a single item, surely a museum has fulfilled its duty to the observer and to the very culture from which the artefact originates?

> *'The unique selling point of a museum is the fact that the public is lured by the opportunity to see the 'real thing' rather than a replica or reproduced image.'*
> 'MUSEUMS MATTER': THE MUSEUM AND GALLERIES COMMISSION.

To consider this skull-cup a treasure is not only testament to its aesthetic beauty but also to its place in a culture rich in history, tradition and belief. Being considered a treasure certainly does not diminish the human remains that make up such an 'artefact', but rather serves to remind the observer that treasure comes in many forms. In the words of a Chinese proverb: 'Learning is a weightless treasure you can always carry easily'.

Kirsty McCarrison

15

PRAYER WHEEL

Silver, turquoise; diameter 7cm, length 22.3cm

China, Tibet, Peshawar Bazaar
20th century CE

Purchased
DUROM.1991.5

The cylinder of this beautiful prayer wheel is silver, decorated in repoussé and set with three turquoises. It was offered to the Oriental Museum in 1990 by a lady, whose husband and son had both graduated from Durham University. She wrote to the curator in August, 'I revisited the Oriental Museum in Durham this weekend and as usual found it one of the most interesting specialist museums I know.' She did not explain how she came to own the prayer wheel, but she particularly wanted it to go to Durham. It was accepted into the collection the following year.

Prayer wheels are quintessentially Tibetan. No other Buddhist culture uses this kind of tool to generate prayers, but Tibetans of every social rank use hand wheels like this one.

Rolls of written prayers, or *mantras*, are sealed inside the cylinder, which is spun with a flick of the wrist. Spinning the wheel brings the same benefits as reading the respective texts and each cycle counts as one repetition of the prayer. As many as forty thousand prayers can be tightly rolled up in the cylinder, so within a few minutes millions of mantras can be 'sent out', and the wheel may be spun for hours. The most common *mantra* is 'om mani padme hum', or 'hail the jewel lotus'.

Mantras are not prayers as westerners understand them, but part of a system of visualizations and recitations aimed at generating the compassion of a *bodhisattva* within oneself. There are many benefits to spinning the wheel with a pure motivation while maintaining proper visualizations and a compassionate mind. *Mantras* can also be repeated to allay everyday fears and anxieties about future rebirths.

There are various kinds of prayer wheel in Tibet. Some are placed on the roofs of houses and turned by the wind; others are powered by running water in rivers and streams, or spun by the hot air rising from lamps and stoves. Large prayer wheels stand in the entrances of temples and are spun by visiting devotees. Together, they radiate endless blessings into the environment: just to be struck by a wind that has touched a prayer wheel cleanses sins and clears obstacles to enlightenment.

Prayer wheels foster a synthesis of body, mind and environment. One Tibetan text from the early 19th century states that the central axis should be made of sandalwood, juniper or another 'non-poisonous' wood, and the ink used to write the *mantras* should be mixed with fragrances, suggesting a fusion of physical and mental purification.

In practice, hand wheels have always varied in quality. A 20th-century prayer wheel might even be made from plastic Pepsi bottles. The spread of new technologies has also led to the development of a more technically advanced method for making a prayer wheel: you can now download the 'om mani padme hum' *mantra* onto your computer's hard drive, where it will spin at fifty-four hundred rotations per minute, calling forth the blessings of the *bodhisattva* as effectively as older technologies of prayer.

Frances Larson

16

MONK'S RICE BOWL

Wood and silver; height 4.5cm, diameter 10cm

China, Tibet
Late 19th or early 20th century CE

Bequest of Professor Helen Muir CBE FRS
DUROM.2006.68

'Treasure, n.: Wealth or riches stored or accumulated, esp. in the form of precious metals; gold or silver coin; hence in general, money, riches, wealth... A store or stock of anything valuable.'

OXFORD ENGLISH DICTIONARY

Whilst westerners tend to associate the word 'treasure' with objects of great financial worth, in many parts of the world the most treasured of objects may also be the most humble. In Buddhist religion the simple rice bowl is imbued with great religious significance and is associated symbolically with the life and teachings of Shakyamuni, (the Sage of the Shakyas) who is commonly known simply as the Historical Buddha.

Shakyamuni was born into a world of wealth and privilege, but rejected his birthright as a prince of the Nepalese Shakya clan in favour of the pursuit of true spiritual enlightenment. Leaving his home at the age of 29, Prince Siddhārtha Gautama travelled widely and studied under several sages. Whilst nearing the point of enlightenment, he sat beneath the Bodhi tree. Whilst so seated, Siddhārtha was mistaken for the spirit of the tree by a young woman named Sujata, who presented him with a golden bowl filled with milk and rice. The young man divided the rice into 49 portions and – because a monk is allowed no grand possessions – flung the golden bowl into a nearby river. He then spent 49 days in meditation, at the end of which he attained the state of enlightenment or *nirvana*.

The humble food bowl thus came to be inextricably linked to the Buddha and his teachings. In the first century CE, images of the Buddha began to be produced in India and many of these featured the perfect holy man in the robes of a monk and cradling a bowl. The rice bowl remains central to the lives of Buddhist monks to this day and is often used to collect the offerings of food and alms upon which they depend for their everyday existence.

Craig Barclay

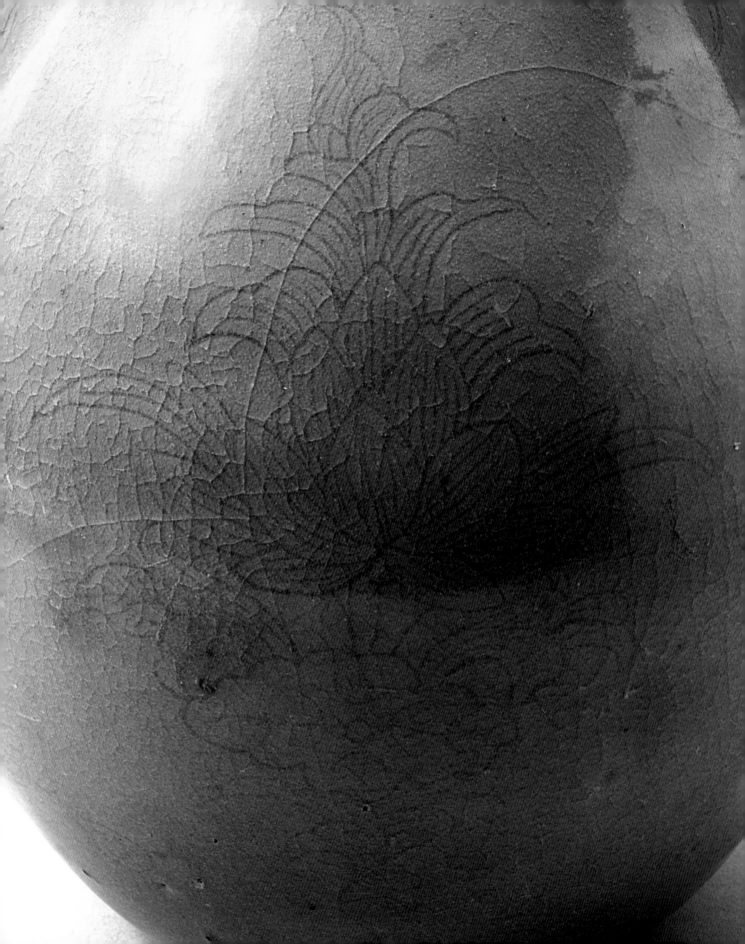

KOREA

Located on a peninsula between the Yellow Sea and the Sea of Japan, Korea is bordered to the northwest by China and the northeast by Russia, with Japan as its other close neighbour across the Korea Strait. Archaeological evidence suggests that the area that now forms Korea was first settled by waves of migrants from southern Siberia in the Neolithic and Bronze ages. Major influences on the early development of Korean culture were the adoption of the Chinese writing system, which took place in the 2nd century BCE, and the introduction of Buddhism in the 4th century CE. In 936 CE King Taejo, founder of the Koryŏ dynasty, created a unified Korea and, despite repeated invasions, this single state continued to exist until 1948 when it was split into North and South Korea at the end of the Korean War.

The Oriental Museum's Korean collection is the smallest of those featured in this book, consisting of just over 300 objects. It is however varied both in terms of dating and content.

Objects within the collection date from the Koryŏ (935–1392 CE) and Choson (1392–1910 CE) dynasties. Notable objects include fine celadon-type glazed stonewares of the Koryŏ dynasty, some undecorated and others featuring underglaze sanggam decoration, such as the one featured in this volume. In addition there are bronze mirrors of the Koryŏ period, and from the Choson dynasty there are musical instruments, textiles and costume, gaming pieces, coins, weapons, furniture and prints.

The collection includes a significant donation from the Right Reverend Richard Rutt, who first travelled to Korea as an Anglican missionary in 1954. Rutt remained in Korea for almost 20 years, serving as Archdeacon of West Seoul from 1965, before becoming Assistant Bishop and then Bishop of the Diocese of Taejon, an area covering several provinces of South Korea. During his time in Korea, Rutt developed a keen interest in the culture and literature of the country and published widely on these subjects in both Korean and English.

Other items come from the collection of Dr Henry de Laszlo. Born in Budapest in 1901 and educated in England and Switzerland, Dr de Laszlo began collecting in 1941 after a visit to the Metropolitan Museum of Art. He feared that the Second World War would result in the destruction of many of the kinds of objects he had seen during that visit and resolved to play his part in preserving what he could. His collection of objects – ranging from Chinese Han Dynasty farm models to bronzes from the Luristan region of Iran – included some very fine Korean ceramic vessels such as the one illustrated in this volume. The collection was loaned to the museum in 1970 by Dr de Laszlo's widow, Mrs Juliane von Hessert, and in 1993 Mrs von Hessert generously agreed to make a gift of much of the collection.

Left: detail of lotus pattern on glazed celadon ewer (no. 18).

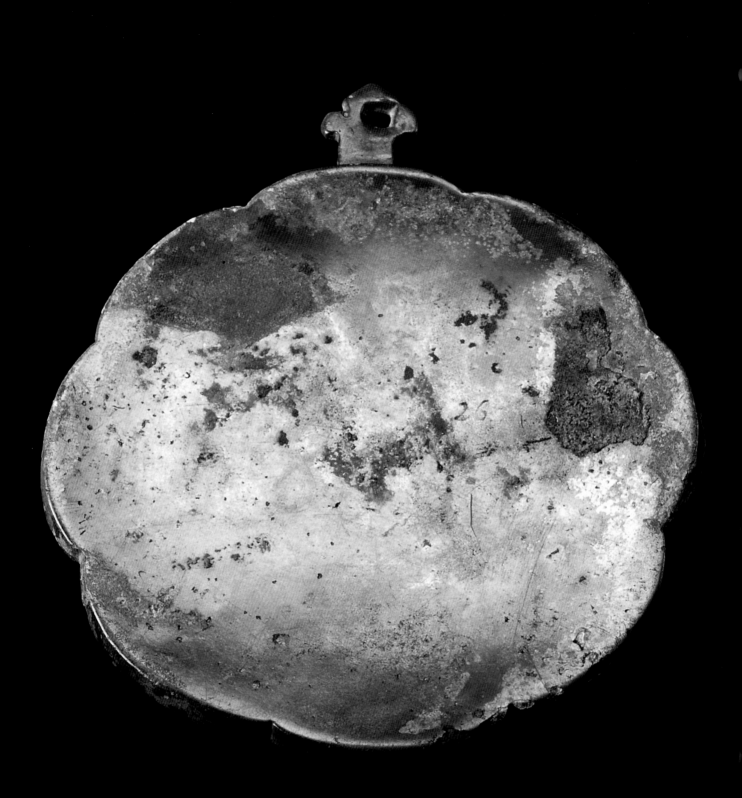

17

Bronze Mirror

Bronze; width 10.2cm, height 12cm

Korea
10th century CE

Gift from Sir Charles Edmund Hardinge
DUROM.1960.4164

Mirrors form a significant sub-section of ancient Korean metalwork, showing off the artistry and imagination of an industry that – like ceramic production – was not ashamed to copy good practice from its Chinese neighbours but could also go its own way. Most of the mirrors now surviving are of the style made for upper class and ritual use in China from the Han (221 BCE–220 CE) to Tang (618–907 CE) dynasties. Typically, these mirrors are circular with a blank and well-polished reflecting face. They were decorated on the reverse with designs that incorporated geometrical, pictorial and calligraphic elements and in later ages they became highly collectable.

Copies were made in both China and Korea: one from the Chinese Qing dynasty (1644–1911 CE) in the Oriental Museum's collection is also shown. It is of the so-called ritual TLV type, incorporating elements into the pattern that resemble these three letters. It also shows an immortal and bears a 42-character inscription referring to him. A raised handling knob in the centre of the reverse side of Chinese mirrors was replaced on Korean mirrors by a pair of small loops through which a carrying cord could be threaded. These loops were sometimes positioned slightly off-centre.

By the 10th century, cheaper mirrors were being made for utilitarian purposes. They were often thinner, had a higher degree of tin in their mineral content that gave them a lighter colour, and were of variable quality. Different shapes appeared; some were square, some were given handles, and Korean shapes included bells. In some examples the eight-lobed floral shape was more pronounced than in the mirror pictured here, and was clearly identifiable as petals. Decoration of the reverse was no longer so important and might be absent altogether, as it seems to have been here.

One side of this mirror is flat, the other slightly concave, and on both sides the surface has deteriorated. A Korean feature was now to locate a suspension loop on the rim. The one seen here is flattened and asymmetrical. Perhaps it was to have assumed a floral shape but was poorly manufactured or damaged in later use. In Korea, mirrors were made at foundries around Kaesŏng and other provincial centres. According to Dr Charlotte Horlyck (SOAS), for whose specialist advice I am grateful, it is impossible to say exactly where or when in the Koryŏ period this mirror was made.

Keith Pratt

Example of a Chinese decorated mirror. DUROM.W44

18

GLAZED GOURD-SHAPED CELADON EWER

Stoneware; height 34.5cm

Korea
Koryŏ Dynasty, 918–1392 CE

Gift from Mrs Juliane von Hessert from the De Laszlo Collection
DUROM.1992.156

From earliest times the Korean peninsula was open to cultural influences from the Chinese mainland – first stonework and metalwork, then the arts of the brush (painting and calligraphy), and eventually technological innovations, including printing and ceramics. In many cases, Koreans took what they learned from China, fused it with native tradition and experience, and created works of art and craftsmanship that were either indistinguishable from top-class Chinese equivalents or deserving of special respect for the fresh insight and development they brought to the form.

Korean potters produced many interesting and individual wares through the first centuries of the first millennium CE, sometimes firing them in long and distinctive 'dragon' kilns that snaked up the hillsides. But it was only in the early Koryŏ dynasty (918–1392 CE) that they began to catch up with the best of contemporary Chinese ceramic wares. Then, features reminiscent of the output from kilns in both northern and southern China began to appear, indicating that refugees from unsettled conditions on the mainland were only too ready to settle down and work with their neighbours on the peninsula. In particular, by the 11th century kilns in south-western Korea were producing good celadons in the style of the *yue* wares from south-east China. Strong encouragement came from the court in Kaesŏng, which associated the pure green shades of celadon glaze with the Buddhist religion that it favoured. Its patronage added to the ready market for fine celadon goods among monasteries and believers across the land.

Overall, Korean potters at this period – like their Chinese peers – tended to emphasize purity of form and colour over more complex shapes and decoration, though water droppers and incense burners nicely modelled in the shape of wildfowl, monkeys and lions showed their appreciation of the natural world. When they did decorate vessels, they frequently drew on natural subjects such as plants, flowers and birds. In time they developed features of their own that were unmatched in China and became greatly admired there. Of special note were *sanggam* wares, celadon vessels inlaid with underglaze designs in white or black slip. These appeared in the first quarter of the 12th century and represent some of the best Korean porcelain of any age.

The ewer in the Oriental Museum collection may belong to the period prior to the appearance of *sanggam*, though a later Koryŏ date cannot be ruled out. It is made in the shape of a double gourd (*pagaji*), with a handle of twisted stems. It may have been used for pouring water into a basin for washing purposes in Buddhist temple rites, in which case the stems would be understood as those of a lotus plant. However, such containers also served as wine vessels, when the handle might suggest a twisted vine. Some similar examples have a lid for attaching with a cord to a loop moulded on top of the handle. Here, there is no lid and no loop, though the glaze covers a stub where the latter would normally be found. As it is not integral to the stem design, this may indicate a failure during the manufacturing process. The lotus pattern was incised before the application of a thickish sage-green glaze, and is repeated on the opposite side of the vessel.

Keith Pratt

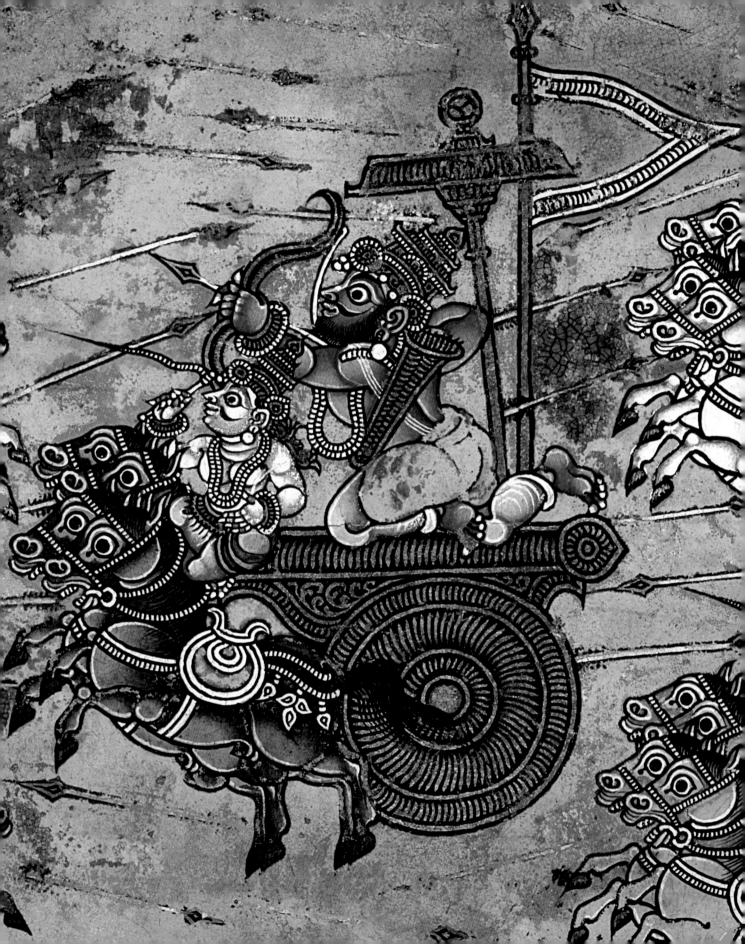

INDIAN SUBCONTINENT

The Indian Subcontinent is defined as the area south of the Himalayas which forms a peninsula extending southwards to the Indian Ocean. The term 'South Asia' is also often used to denote an area which includes not only the modern states of India, Pakistan and Bangladesh, but can also be considered to encompass Nepal, Bhutan and the island of Sri Lanka. Overall, South Asia encompasses an area of around 4.4 million square kilometres.

The first known permanent settlements in the area date to more than 9,000 years ago and these developed into the Indus Valley Civilisation from the 4th millennium BCE. Four of the world's major religions – Hinduism, Buddhism, Jainism and Sikhism – originated here; and Christianity, Islam, Judaism and Zoroastrianism have also helped to shape the rich and diverse culture of the region as they arrived along the important trade routes that cross the country. The history of the area is one of vast empires, huge wealth and great diversity. This is reflected in the rich and varied art and archaeology of the region.

The 1,500 objects comprising the Oriental Museum's Indian collections reflect all of the major religions that have shaped the region's culture. They range in scope from sculpture in stone to furniture, textiles, arms and armour, manuscripts and paintings. Of particular importance are an exquisite group of miniature paintings and a fine collection of Mughal jade. There is also a very significant collection of Gandharan sculpture which reflect the exchange of ideas between the Indian Subcontinent and Hellenic Europe. Examples from all of these collections feature in this volume.

In addition, the museum holds a set of nearly 5,000 photographs of archaeological sites and monuments made between 1902 and 1923 by Sir John Marshall, Director General of Archaeology in India. This archive provides an important resource for those studying India's architectural and archaeological heritage, offering unique images of many structures and features which have since been lost.

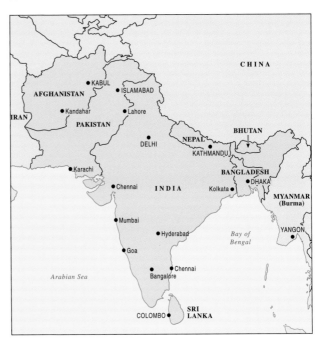

Left: detail of illustration from Mahabharata *manuscript (no. 20).*

THE DURHAM BODHISATTVA

Grey schist; height 21cm

Pakistan (Kingdom of Gandhara)
2nd century CE

Gift from the Rt Hon Malcolm MacDonald
DUROM.1969.346

The Durham *Bodhisattva's* head is oval and centred on a long, narrow nose within a well-preserved face. His eyes are prominently defined as thin slits between sharply-cut upper and lower eyelids and a prominent *urna* is carved in high relief above the bridge of his nose. Both ears are visible and whilst the left is broken, the right is long, concave and oblique to the head. The nose terminates in a filtrum above pronounced, raised lips and a thin, wavy moustache which extends across both cheeks towards the ears. The *Bodhisattva's* hair undulates to the sides with a distinct peak over the forehead secured by a band of three strings of square beads punctuated at the front by thick rounded spacers. The exposed right-hand side of the band is also interrupted, but with a thin spherical bead on either side of the spacers. The hair immediately above and below the band takes a distinct chevron form but rises to a central chignon with retaining knot supporting three thick loops, one to the right, one to the left and one towards the back of the head. The base of the neck is roughly fractured and damage to the reverse of the head suggests the presence of a large, flat halo framing the entire head.

These features indicate that the Durham *Bodhisattva* belongs to the corpus of Buddhist schist statues from the ancient territory of Gandhara, which lay north of the Indus and south of the Pamirs. This region, also known as the Crossroads of Asia, witnessed the exchange and mixing of many different cultural impulses under the patronage of the Kushan Emperors. Here Indic philosophy was mixed with Hellenistic and Greco-Roman traditions of sculpture to produce some of the earliest attempts to depict the Gautama *Buddha* in the first century of the Common Era. Carving from soft schist, Gandhara's sculptors soon began to facilitate the introduction of a new Mahayana philosophical development – the *Bodhisattva*. Unlike the Gautama Buddha, who had achieved *nirvana*, an ultimate state of nothingness, and was unable to intercede on the behalf of those in need, the Mahayana conceptualised a powerful, princely figure who had achieved enlightenment, but whose worldly role was solely to assist others obtain bliss. The Durham *Bodhisattva* epitomises established strength and wealth and would have created a striking contrast with the increasingly less popular plain and unadorned statues of the Gautama Buddha. A mass cult by the 4th and 5th centuries CE with smaller examples enshrined in domestic chapels across Gandhara, it may be deduced that the Durham *Bodhisattva* was a key icon in a major shrine. Presumed to represent the Maitreya *Buddhisattva* or future *Buddha*, devotees would have eagerly anticipated His Coming when, in the words of their teachers, the present age will end in flames and all sentient beings will:

'lose their doubts, and the torrents of their cravings will be cut off: free from all misery they will manage to cross the ocean of becoming... No longer will they regard anything as their own, they will have no possession, no gold or silver, no home, no relatives... They will have torn the net of the passions, they will manage to enter into trances, and theirs will be an abundance of joy and happiness, for they will lead a holy life under Maitreya's guidance.'

Robin Coningham and Christopher Davis

MAHABHARATA MANUSCRIPT

Ink, opaque watercolour and gilt on paper; length 40cm, width 22cm

India, Karnataka, Srirangapatna
1669 CE

Purchase
DUROM.1964.17

The *Mahabharata* or 'great story of the Bharatas' is, at its very core, a family story. It revolves around the Kauravas and Pandavas, senior and junior branches respectively of the Kuru ruling family of Hastinapur, and the inevitable conflict which ensues in their bid to secure the Kuru throne.

This fragment depicts a scene from the *Drona parva* or Book of Drona, which tells the story of the second and major part of the epochal battle of Kurukshetra. Fragments of descriptive text surround a central illustration depicting three of the five Pandava brothers (Bhima at centre, Arjuna at top right, and Yudishthira at bottom right) as they let fly their arrows towards their opponents the Kauravas. The two figures on the left are described as *Don* or *Dron senya*, translating to Drona's soldiers or army. As Drona was the second commander of the Kaurava forces, they can be taken to represent the Kaurava army. For argument's sake, perhaps we see Drona himself, who in more peaceful times was teacher to both the Pandava and Kaurava cousins, conceivably accompanied by Duryodhana, the eldest of the 99 Kaurava brothers.

The illustration superbly captures the energy and momentum of battle, with horses, chariots, people and arrows all leaping out of the frame and tilted towards one another at occasionally crazy angles as they career over a red battlefield bloodied and littered with thousands of dead. By the time it ended, the battle of Kurukshetra annihilated nearly all its participants, initially through fair and later through foul play, leaving only the Pandavas and about five other characters to survive the carnage.

The other noteworthy figure in the illustration is Arjuna's blue- or dark-skinned charioteer, instantly recognisable as Krishna. Cousin, friend and chief strategist of the Pandavas, he is also an incarnation of the Hindu god Vishnu (the preserver aspect of the Hindu trinity). At the start of battle Krishna soothes Arjuna's despair at waging war on his own family and friends by discussing the nature of human goals, the importance of doing one's duty, and the relationship of the individual to society and the world. This section of the story is known as the *Bhagavad Gita* or 'The Lord's song' and is believed to contain the essentials of Hindu philosophy – hence its elevation as *the* book of Hinduism, although sole allegiance to it is not actually required by the religion.

Written in Sanskrit and at nearly one hundred thousand verses, the *Mahabharata* is one of the longest poems in the world, and is about four times the length of the Ramayana (or 'story of Rama'), the second of India's great epics. Both are of immense cultural significance but the *Mahabharata's* famous claim at the outset that, 'What is found here, may be found elsewhere; what is not found here, will not be found elsewhere' provides a clue to its special nature. For it encompasses all of human life – from the complexity of our relationships and the choices we make, to the depths of our emotion, and the luminosity of our intellect when expressed through philosophy. Expanded from a 7th-8th century BCE poem originally called *Jaya* or 'Victory', its rootedness in centuries past is no deterrent to it being easily understood today. To paraphrase a popular saying, it has something in it for everyone.

Mrinalini Venkateswaran

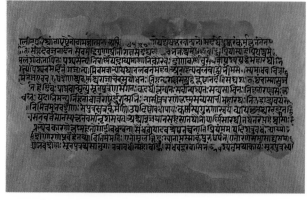

Reverse of manuscript page.

21

KHANJAR (KNIFE) HILT

Jade, with cloisonné enamel decoration; length 13.1cm, width 6cm

Mughal India and China
1675 to 1725 CE

Gift from Sir Charles Edmund Hardinge
DUROM.1960.3599

The carved white nephrite jade hilt is of characteristic Mughal *khanjar* form with a bulbous pommel. The fine quality jade is decorated with cloisonné enamel arranged in floral decoration in turquoise blue, dark blue, red and green. The remains of two iron pins at the end of the hilt indicate that a blade would have been attached to form the original knife (*khanjar*).

This *khanjar* hilt is one of a group of exquisite Mughal jade carvings held by the Oriental Museum. This piece adheres to the principles of Islamic art, being abstract in design, with a wealth of rich decoration: a design that avoids human or animal representation. The piece also reflects the luxuriousness and great refinement of the Mughals. This luxury is, of course, also to be found in the Taj Mahal built by Shah Jahan for his wife Mumtaz-i Mahal in 1629, the most famous monument of Mughal architecture.

The Mughal dynasty was founded by Zahar al-Dan (reigned 1526–1550), who in turn claimed descent from the great Central Asian ruler Timur (Tamerlane). By the late 16th century most of India was ruled by the powerful Mughal empire, with its distinct Indian-Islamic culture. The empire was ruled by a sequence of despotic monarchs including Akhbar (1555–1605), Jahangir (1605–1627), Shah Jahan (1627–1658) and Aurangzeb (1658–1707) but after Aurangzeb died the empire went into rapid decline and suffered a crippling invasion by Nadir Shah of Persia in 1739. 1761 marks the dividing line between the Mughal and British periods of rule in India, though the Mughal empire continued to exist in name until 1858.

Jade carving first developed in fine form in India during Emperor Jahangir's rule (1605–1627) and continued throughout the 17th and 18th centuries at the Mughal court. The Durham *khanjar* hilt was produced between 1675 and 1725. The best work would have been produced at leisure to supply wealthy princes and nobles, with craftsmen occupying a secure place in Mughal urban hierarchies and often being organised into guilds. Many of the craftsmen learned their skills from their forefathers and each group of craftsmen belonged to a separate caste. The courts supported artisans, enabling them to produce high-quality artefacts: court patronage was an important aspect of political life in the Mughal empire. Highly-decorated weapons were used purely for ceremonial purposes as symbols of dignity and political status. They were often given as gifts from a ruler to his subordinates in return for political allegiances.

The piece is additionally significant as it demonstrates a flow of art and trade between India and China, for the handle's brass and blue enamel inlay are Chinese. The cloisonné decoration imitates typical Mughal craftsmanship, which was characterised by the highly skilled use of turquoise, meticulously-set precious stones and gold. It is likely that, in this case, a blank handle was sent to China for decoration, although jade pieces produced in India during the 18th and 19th centuries often betray heavy Turkish and Chinese influences. Luxury Indian jade items were similarly imported into China from the late 16th century and workmen imitated the perfection of Mughal pieces in the palace workshops there. Conversely, the early Mughals favoured imports from Persia and China and the impetus for these crafts may initially have come from China, Central Asia or Persia.

Janet Starkey

22

Jewelled Necklace

Gold, diamonds, rubies, emeralds and pearls; length 9cm, width 13.5cm

India
19th century CE

Bequest of Professor Helen Muir CBE FRS
DUROM.2006.65

Within the context of a museum collection, the term 'Treasure' is frequently granted to an item of exceptional cultural importance or outstanding beauty. All museum objects however come endowed with a web of associations and connections which can serve to elevate even a relatively modest artefact above the level of the mundane. Often such associations take the form of links to the individuals who collected, used or wore the artefacts under consideration. In such cases, the story of the person can be even more fascinating than the tale of the object.

Professor Helen Muir, the daughter of a senior official in the Indian Civil Service, was born in August 1920. Following the birth, Muir's mother was urged by the Maharajah of Jaipur not to be disappointed at having borne a daughter rather than a son. In the light of Professor Muir's subsequent career, it is clear that such concerns were misplaced. The tiny baby was destined to grow up to be one of the most distinguished British scientists of her generation.

Schooled at Downe House in Newbury, the ambitious Muir secured a place at Somerville College, Oxford, where she studied chemistry under the Nobel laureate Dorothy Hodgkin. Following her graduation in 1944, she embarked upon doctoral research in the field of biochemistry prior to taking up a post at the National Institute for Medical Research in 1948. Developing a keen interest in arthritis and cartilage, her career followed an upward trajectory, culminating in her appointment to the directorship of the Kennedy Institute for Rheumatology at Hammersmith in West London. Universally acknowledged as a leader in her field, Muir developed an international team of collaborators who were affectionately known as 'Helen's bag carriers'. The significance of her contributions to the study of osteoarthritis were recognised throughout the world and British honours – including her appointment as a Fellow of the Royal Society in 1977; as a CBE in 1981; and the receipt of numerous honorary degrees – were mirrored by her being granted Membership of the Royal Swedish Academy of Sciences in 1989.

Throughout her life Professor Muir maintained an exceptionally keen interest in riding and hunting, even using data gathered through her study of the stresses placed on the joints and bones of foxhounds to inform her researches into human disease. She frequently rode with the Percy Hunt in Northumbria, and on one memorable occasion was amused to find herself mistaken by the press for the young Lady Diana Spencer whilst leaving Alnwick Castle. Professor Muir's regular visits to the North East led her to identify the Oriental Museum as a suitable home for the collection of Chinese and Indian artefacts which decorated her home near Bedale in North Yorkshire. The collection which she ultimately bequeathed to the museum included textiles, fine Chinese ceramics and sculptural stonework. The most spectacular of the pieces were however the examples of fine Indian jewellery which recalled her birth and early childhood in South Asia. These included a stunning gold necklace, set with 40 diamonds, 38 rubies, 27 emeralds and seven pearls. Most of the Indian alluvial diamonds appear to have been locally cut, but three are faceted in a characteristically European style.

Craig Barclay

Helen Muir's certificate of membership of the Royal Swedish Academy of Sciences.

12 Goddesses.

Painting of Twelve Goddesses

23

Ink, opaque watercolour and gilt on paper; length 35.5cm, width 25cm

India, Rajasthan
1850–1899 CE

Purchase
DUROM.1962.256

The long history and close association of India's many indigenous faiths has led to a great deal of syncretism among them. Jainism and Hinduism thus naturally share a philosophical, artistic, literary and architectural vocabulary exemplified for instance by the influence of the Jain concept of *ahimsa* (avoidance of violence) on Hindu philosophy, or the presence of variations of originally Hindu divinities such as *Saraswati* or *Kali* in the Jain pantheon.

The style of the painting conforms to a broader trend throughout Rajasthan which evolved out of the close association of the Rajasthani courts with the popular Mughal style at Delhi. This initially saw the 'rough-and-ready' Rajasthani styles adopt elements of the more sophisticated Mughal miniature tradition. However, by the middle of the 19th century, artists had become adept at catering to varied audiences. Not only did artists situated within Mughal and Rajasthani courts draw from both painting traditions, but they also created various levels of work – for instance creating both refined works for courtly viewing and 'mass-produced' paintings for wider circulation.

The appearance of several subjects on a single surface divided into various registers, as seen here, is a typically Jain style of illustration, evident from the earliest surviving Jain texts on paper from about the 15th century CE. The colours used in this instance suggest an affiliation with the Jaipur school of painting, in some ways the longest and most heavily influenced by the Mughal court as a result of Jaipur being one of the first Rajput kingdoms to ally itself with the Mughals. All the motifs used in the painting are derived from Mughal sources, while the costumes and ornaments are typical of Rajasthan. However, since the subject matter is of Jain divinities, the strict adherence to their associated iconography maintained in all Jain art (i.e. the various implements carried by the goddesses, and their mounts), is also seen here. Interestingly, by the 19th century such compartmentalised paintings on cardboard were a product of the Jaipur area being used by artists to illustrate a wide variety of subjects ranging from divinities to architecture.

Paintings in the Jaipur area are traditionally executed on cloth or paper, or additionally on walls. The range of papers includes a heavy, cardboard-like paper extensively produced in the paper manufacturing centre of Sanganer in Jaipur state well into the 20th century, which makes the cardboard base of this particular example somewhat unusual. However, the increasing demand from Europeans and tourists meant that miniatures were quickly produced and artists were open to experimenting with diverse media. The painting otherwise adheres to the traditional technique of miniature paintings executed on paper, where a *wasli* or base (here cardboard) is first prepared and then coated with *safeda* or zinc oxide before proceeding to the actual application of colour. The colours that appear are largely mineral and plant-based and here include *hinglu* (vermillion or mercury red, especially at the borders), *asmani* (sky or lapis blue for the clouds), *neel* (indigo or dark blue), *danafarang* (light green), *savapankhi* (parrot or dark green), *mungia* (dark green), *peori* (yellow), *sindur* (orange) and *syahi* (lamp black).

Mrinalini Venkateswaran, Sonika Soni and Dipti Khera

The names of the goddesses from left to right and top to bottom where decipherable are: "Shri Yakesvari Devi Ji (1)", "Shri Shrajiva Devi Ji (2)", "Shri Dutari/ Dulari Devi Ji (3)", "Shri Kali Devi Ji (4)", "Shri Kavla/ Kamla Devi Ji (5)", "Shri Shyama Devi Ji (6)", "Shri Sachanand Devi Ji (7)", "Shri Brakuti Devi Ji (8)", "Shri Sutara Devi Ji (9)", "Shri Asopa Devi Ji (10)", "Shri Manbo Devi Ji (11)", "Shri [...]da Devi Ji (12)".

JAPAN

Japan is actually an archipelago made up of more than 4,000 islands. The four largest islands, from north to south, are Hokkaido, Honshu, Shikoku, and Kyushu and together these make up 97% of the land mass around which the many other smaller islands cluster. Most of the islands are mountainous and many are volcanic.

Evidence for human occupation of the islands dates back for many thousands of years and the early Jomon culture (approximately 10,000 BCE to around 400 BCE) has produced some of the oldest surviving examples of pottery found in the world. Japan is first mentioned in Chinese histories in 57 CE and contact with China and Korea has had a significant influence on the development of Japanese culture since this point. However, Japan's island status has allowed it to maintain independence, and at times isolation, from the outside world and permitted a highly distinctive culture to flourish.

The Japanese collections at the Oriental Museum are the largest in number after the Chinese and Egyptian collections. They mostly date from the Edo (1615–1868) and Meiji (1868–1912) periods, but with some objects from earlier periods such as the Muromachi (1336–1573) and Momoyama (1573–1615). There are significant numbers of objects of 20th and increasingly, even 21st, century date.

In material terms, the collection is quite diverse though the best represented areas are textiles, arms and armour, ceramics, woodblock prints, *inro*, and *netsuke*. Other items include domestic shrines, furniture, lacquer ware of various types, paintings, dolls, statues, games and gaming pieces, bronze temple bells, coins, and lantern slides.

Among the highlights of the Japanese collections are the Edo period *ukiyo-e* (floating world) woodblock prints with images of actors, courtesans, and landscapes, by renowned artists such as Ando Hiroshige (1797–1858) and Katsushika Hokusai (1760–1849).

The museum also has an exquisite album of woodblock prints, entitled *Shin Bijin*, by the Meiji period artist Toyohara Chikanobu (1838–1912). Other highlights include fine examples of swords and armour, finely embroidered silk *kimono* and exquisitely carved *netsuke*, finely decorated *inro*, as well as *imari* ceramics of the 17th and 18th centuries.

Unlike many other collections in the museum, the Japanese collections were not built up as the result of one or two major donations. Instead they are the result of many smaller gifts from a large number of generous individuals and a considerable number of purchases.

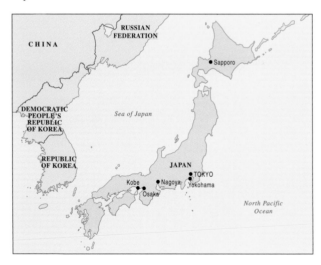

Left: inro and netsuke (no. 26).

Bronze Buddha Head

24

Bronze; height 51cm, width 27cm, depth 28cm

Japan
Kamakura Period, about 1185–1333 CE

Gift from Sir Charles Edmund Hardinge
DUROM.1960.811

A powerhouse of the industrialised world, Japan is home to legions of sophisticated robots: the world's largest fleet of mechanized workers, some dexterous enough to be pick up a grain of rice. It was also the original home of this ancient bronze Buddha head. Created in about 1300 CE, it is exquisitely cast, chased and patinated with a delicate shade of pale slate green/grey. This head would have originally formed part of a large seated figure of the Buddha Shakyamuni placed in a temple.

Buddhism was introduced to Japan from Korea, becoming the dominant religion under Empress Suiko (593–623 CE). The resulting temples and monasteries created a demand for bronze Buddha figures, bronze being more durable than stone or copper. These figures began as Chinese in style, but by the Kamakura period (about 1185–1333 CE), they had developed a distinctively Japanese character.

The term Buddha itself refers to the Buddha Shakyamuni, who is said to be the only Buddha to *appear* in the world. He was born as Prince Siddhārtha Gautama, the eldest son and heir to the ruler of a small city state on the border of northern India. Struck by the meaninglessness of his life he was moved to give up his kingdom, leaving his wife and young son. He renounced wealth, privilege and worldly life to seek the causes of human suffering. After achieving enlightenment under the Bodhi tree, he went into a deep meditation for seven days.

The small, curl-like forms seen on the Buddha's head are actually snails, which covered the Buddha's head thereby protecting him from the scorching sun during his seven-day meditation. They have been immortalized along with the Buddha. The head crowned by the martyred snails (sometimes mistaken for hair) also boasts something resembling a topknot. This protuberance, called the *Usnisa*, is not a turban or topknot but is one of the legendary *Mahapurusha Lakshanas* that mark out an enlightened master.

Eventually, in search of his own Path, the Buddha Shakyamuni went to the Himalayas where he meditated for six years whilst practicing the extreme asceticism of eating only a single grain of rice and a single sesame seed each day. An interesting image springs to mind of a contemporary mechanized worker feeding a grain of rice to the ancient Buddha!

The generic round face with its abundant look is not present in this bronze Buddha. Not idealized in the same way as some of its predecessors, the features show the character of a human being. The atypical long face with its square jaw, broad nose and thin lips looks as though it belongs to an actual person. Is this because it represents the only *living* Buddha? The gigantic ears make the already extremely thin neck look even thinner, whilst the symbolically long earlobes which once containing jewels are a reminder that Prince Gautama was formerly dragged down by wealth. How the Durham head came to be separated from the body of the sculpture it originally topped must remain a mystery, but it is possible that the delicate neck ultimately proved unable to support the weight of the heavy bronze head.

Jane McAdam Freud

25

Shino Ware Tea-Bowl

Pottery; height 7.7cm, diameter 11cm

Japan
Azuchi-Momoyama Period, 1574–1600 CE

Purchased
DUROM.1978.112

Although the Tea Ceremony is for many people synonymous with Japanese culture, the tea plant itself is not native to Japan. First introduced from China during the 9th century CE, it was not, however, until about 1187 that a new type of powdered green tea called *matcha* was imported by Eisai Zenji from the Buddhist monasteries of China. Eisai Zenji is also credited with introducing Zen Buddhism to Japan, and for importing the original tea seeds which gave birth to Uji's renowned tea fields.

Originally used by monks as a medicine and meditative stimulant, the consumption of tea was later adopted by secular society. This use in turn evolved by the late 15th century CE into *Chado* (the Way of Tea), as the aesthetic consideration of Japan's social elite melded with Zen spirituality. From this confluence a new aesthetic – *wabi* – emerged, which rejected waste and extravagance. Instead, *wabi* celebrated natural simplicity, imperfection, and irregularity. This veneration of simple and unadorned objects was eloquently manifested in the production of the bowls used in the Tea Ceremony.

During the late 16th century CE numerous new kilns were established in Mino Province by potters fleeing unrest elsewhere in Japan. A distinctive product of the new Mino kilns was Shino Ware (志野焼 *Shino-yaki*), which was produced in the area around Seto.

Shino Ware was made from clay which contained a low percentage of iron and which fired to a pale colour. The bodies of the pots were covered with a white felspathic glaze. Shino Ware vessels are generally fairly squat, and whilst thickly potted, are surprisingly light in weight. They were characterised by thick white crawling glazes (a by-product of having been fired over a long period at a relatively low temperature) and by numerous microscopic holes in the surface of the glaze.

Examples which display red staining were particularly highly prized by tea masters, who referred to the staining as 'fire colour' (*hi-iro*) or 'scorch' (*koge*). Amongst the most popular types of Shino Ware vessel was the *chawan* (tea-bowl). The Durham specimen is of an irregular form known in Japanese as *kutsu gata* (shoe-shaped). A crack in the body of the bowl has been filled by a previous owner using gold lacquer: an eloquent testament to the high regard in which the *chawan* was held.

'To empty one's mind is to forget the self. To forget the self is to awaken to the world. To awaken to everything in the world is to be enlightened.'

Dogen Zenji (1200–1253)

Craig Barclay

26

INRO AND NETSUKE

Lacquer and cord; inro length 9.2cm, width 4.5cm, netsuke diameter 3.5cm

Japan
Edo Period, 1750–1799 CE

Gift from Mrs E Humphreys-Owens
DUROM.1970.64

The earliest links between Japan and North East England developed in the mid-19th century following the signing of the Treaty of Amity and Commerce in 1858. This allowed certain ports in Japan to open to British trade and thus began diplomatic and trading relations between Japan and the UK.

Various Japanese delegations later took the opportunity to visit the UK and learn the ways of the West in order to bring modernisation to Japan. The most famous of these was the Iwakura Mission. This mission travelled to Newcastle in 1872 to observe the production of weapons and the construction of ships. The delegates were so impressed that the Japanese navy would later start commissioning the construction of warships at various Tyneside shipyards.

The construction of these ships inevitably brought Japanese sailors to live in the Tyneside area, and in some cases they married local women and settled permanently, helping to create a small Japanese community. From 1914 onwards, Japan developed its own shipbuilding industry and later, due to the strains of World War Two, the relationship between the region and Japan was severed. However, friendship was renewed again in the 1950s when Crown Prince (now Emperor) Akihito visited the North East when he came to the UK in 1953 to attend the Queen's coronation.

From the 1970s, Japan has reinvigorated its relationship with the North East of England. A number of Japanese companies have invested in the region over the years, Nissan being the most significant. The year 2008 marked the 150th anniversary of the signing of the Treaty of Amity and Commerce and was celebrated with a programme of events called *Japan-UK 150*. It is not without significance that this coincided with the Oriental Museum sending many of its finest artefacts on an extended multi-venue tour of Japan.

During 2008 many diverse events were held in the North East of England and helped ensure the continuing friendship and mutual understanding between the people of Japan and the North East of England. Nowhere is this understanding better demonstrated than in Durham University's Oriental Museum, where exquisite artefacts from Japan have served as an inspiration to generations of British students.

One such treasure is a magnificent lacquered case, or *inro*, decorated with scenes illustrating part of the 53 stages of the road from Edo (the modern Tokyo) to Kyoto. Signed Kaji-Kawa and bearing the seal of Yoshi-Chika, it represents an exquisite example of Japanese craftsmanship. An *inro* of this quality would have been worn by a man of wealth as a means of carrying his small personal possessions. Hung from the waist, it was in effect a small nested box, its tiny individual compartments performing the same function as the pockets of a European jacket or trousers. The *inro* retains its original cord, slider-bead (*ojime*) and the toggle (*netsuke*) which would have allowed it to be hung from its owner's waist-sash. Overall it is a magnificent piece: a beautifully-preserved and highly evocative reminder of the costumes and customs which prevailed in Japan prior to the importation and adoption of western styles of dress.

Hideaki Yokohama

HIROSHIGE WOODBLOCK PRINT

Rice-paper; length 35.5cm, width 23cm

Japan
Edo Period,1857 CE

Purchase from Mr GW Vaughn-Hughes
DUROM.1962.28

Hiroshige's woodblock print *Takanawa Ushimachi* is truly a treasure in that it offers a unique vision of Japanese culture, which we grasp visually rather than verbally. The focus of the print is the enlarged cartwheel, which leads the viewer's eye to the rainbow looming over a tranquil sea. Floating in the sea are sailboats that gradually disappear into the distant pink horizon. The delicate gradations of the blue sea lead the viewer back to shore in the foreground.

Mikhail Uspensky, a Hiroshige expert, suggests that the seemingly random objects in the foreground are in fact symbolic, offering the viewer a puzzle to ponder. The enlarged cartwheel personifies the title *Ushimachi*, meaning 'the Ox Quarter'. Carts drawn by oxen were reserved for members of high nobility in the Japanese hierarchy and occasionally for construction in the city of Edo. The straw-coloured sandal being toyed with by the animals suggests the end of a long journey, while the watermelon rinds signify the end of summer and transition to autumn. The transitory symbolism in the foreground creates a feeling of serenity and intimacy.

The minimized background and enlarged foreground not only serve to provide perspective but also to bring the viewer into an experience of nature with its various moods. This use of perspective, originally a western technique, was used in Japan as a way of making hyper-realistic images. Hiroshige customized this western idea of perspective by contrasting passive elements in the background with the more symbolic figures in the foreground. Dr Smith of Harvard University suggests that due to the contrasting moods of the background and foreground, Hiroshige's prints should be read from back to front. This new take on western technique in turn inspired late 19th- and 20th-century European impressionists and post-impressionists such as Whistler, Cezanne and Gauguin to approach landscapes in a similar way.

Caitlin McInnis

Carving in Ivory of Weaver and Family

Ivory; length 15cm, width 5cm, height 6.5cm

Japan
1913 CE

Gift from Mrs Lesley Lewis through The Art Fund
DUROM.2006.91

The Art Fund is the UK's leading independent art charity, entirely funded through the support of its 80,000 members. It campaigns on behalf of museums and their visitors, promotes the enjoyment of art and, most significantly, helps UK museums and galleries enrich their collections. Since its foundation in 1903, the charity has helped more than 600 museums and galleries all over the UK secure over 870,000 works of art for their permanent collections.

The Art Fund is perhaps best known for offering grants towards acquisitions (offering around £4 million annually), but it also acts as a conduit for lifetime gifts and bequests of works of art. For example, in 1955 Ernest E Cook (grandson of Thomas Cook, founder of the travel company) chose to bequeath his extensive collection of fine and decorative art to The Art Fund for distribution to museums throughout the UK. More recently Professor Sir Colin St John Wilson made a lifetime gift of his collection of iconic 20th-century works to Pallant House Gallery through The Art Fund.

The donors who choose to present works are many and varied, including not only major collectors and well-known philanthropists, but also individuals of more modest means but with a discerning eye. Many donors give primarily to support The Art Fund's work making great art available for everyone to enjoy, but there are also other considerable advantages to channelling a gift in this way.

Given its long experience and UK-wide range of grant-giving, The Art Fund has a detailed and comprehensive knowledge of public collections and their collecting priorities – essential to identify the most appropriate (and not always the most obvious) home for a particular object. Every object offered is assessed by The Art Fund's Trustees, who apply the same criteria as when assessing requests for financial support: the work must be of good museum quality.

Any work given or bequeathed to a museum through The Art Fund is subject to a set of binding terms and conditions, which ensure that the work will be well cared for in perpetuity and not disposed of. The work must also remain accessible to the public, and the donor's contribution must be acknowledged, along with that of The Art Fund. These conditions provide great comfort to donors in a period of intense pressure on resources and uncertainty about the long-term future of many museums.

In addition, since The Art Fund is a registered charity, the value of any work bequeathed is deducted from the donor's estate before any inheritance tax liability is calculated.

One of the finest of the pieces on display in Durham is remarkable not for its size but for its exquisite beauty and matchless craftsmanship. Presented to the museum by Mrs Lesley Lewis via The Art Fund, this tiny treasure takes the form of a carved ivory figure group of mat-weavers. It provides a vivid image of 19th-century Japanese life. A man sits cross-legged on a rolled-up mat at one end of a long table, with a long thread in his hand. At the other end of the table a young girl in a butterfly kimono crouches on one knee and grasps at the hem of the long garment worn by a younger child who crawls purposefully across the table-top. It is a beautiful portrayal of family life, but it also provides the viewer with a unique three-dimensional image of work in a Japanese mat-weaver's workshop.

The true brilliance of the ivory-carver is betrayed by the care taken to portray the everyday tools of the weaver's trade. Two tools lie to one side of the table-top and a roll of decorative ribbon together with a bundle of threads or fibres wrapped in a mat to the other. Under the table – and thus hidden from the eye of the casual viewer – lie a rule and a bag of tools. Small but perfect in every way: this truly is a treasure to behold.

Sophie Harrison and Craig Barclay

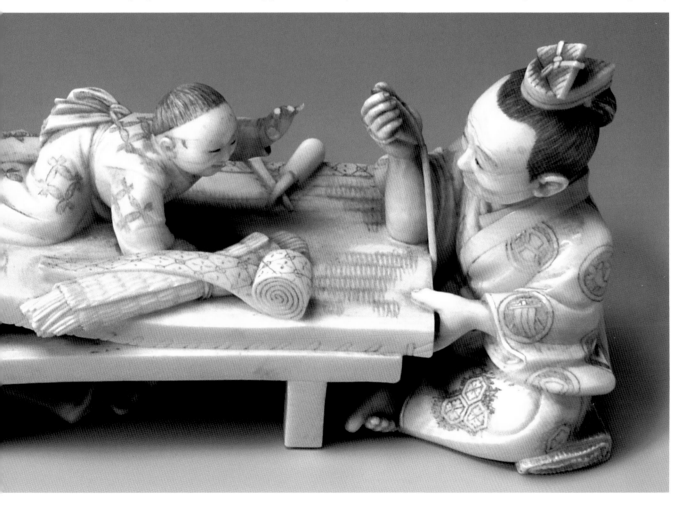

SOUTH EAST ASIA

South East Asia is made up of two distinct geographic regions: the tip of the Asian mainland; and then the islands and archipelagos that stretch away from it. The mainland section consists of Cambodia, Laos, Myanmar (Burma), Thailand, Vietnam and peninsular Malaysia. The islands include East Malaysia, the Philippines, Brunei and Singapore.

Standing as they do in the shadow of India and China, the countries of South East Asia have been greatly influenced by these larger neighbours. From India and the Middle East they have adopted Hinduism, Buddhism and Islam; together with legal and medical knowledge; distinctive artistic and architectural styles; textile manufacturing; and metal-working techniques. From China have come Confucianism, Taoism and other strands of Buddhism; ceramic and lacquer-working techniques; silk-making; financial and medical practices; and alternative styles of art and architecture. All of these influences have been absorbed, mixed and adapted to create a series of linked but distinctive cultures.

The South East Asian collections at the Oriental Museum reflect the diverse nature of this area. The museum is home to collections from the majority of the countries listed above and the objects range from ceramics to textiles, as well as including musical instruments, wood carvings, lacquer-ware and arms and armour. The museum is also home to the Javanese gamelan owned by the Music Department of Durham University and visitors to the museum can hear the gamelan being played most Wednesday afternoons.

The core of the South East Asian collections is formed by the objects acquired in two groups in 1976 and 1980 from Malcolm MacDonald. After World War II, MacDonald served first as Governor General of Malaya and Singapore and later as Commissioner General for South East Asia. Ever the collector, during this time he amassed a considerable number of fascinating pieces which reflect the cultures of the region. Many of these objects, such as the xylophone and sword featured in this section, were presented to him by key political figures in the region at that time.

Complementing this is the Roberts Collection of Balinese art. This substantial collection of woodcarving, sculpture and paintings from the island of Bali provides a detailed picture of the changing nature of art on the island during the 20th century.

Left: detail from a Balinese wood carving showing a scene from the Ramayana (no. 32).

29

Burmese Manuscript Chest

Wood, gold leaf, lacquer and glass; height 126.5cm, length 173cm, width 92cm

Myanmar (Burma)
19th century CE

Purchase
DUROM.GQ155

This manuscript chest (*sadaik* in Burmese), originates from the State of Myanmar (formerly Burma) and is a typical but magnificent example of chests made in this region during the late 18th and early 19th centuries. The chest is made from Burmese teak, *thayo* (relief moulded) with black lacquer and gilded panelling to three sides. It is decorated with scenes from the Buddha's life on the main panel; whilst on the side panels a floral scrollwork border surrounds double images containing Buddhist symbols. It was most likely made near or in Mandalay, where craftsmen specialized in making relief patterns in lacquer. Relief-moulded lacquer chests of this sort represented a fine art form in Mandalay and were created for the storage of Buddhist literature and secular documents.

Chests such as this were used as repositories for cultural knowledge in Myanmar and Thailand, and stored texts on subjects including Buddhism, sociology, history and astrology. The magnificence of the decoration on the chests is testament to the strong tradition of honouring education in the region. According to Khur-yearn, chests are still widely used both in homes and monasteries for storing literature, but the tradition of producing manuscripts is dying out. Traditionally, shorter manuscripts were made of palm-leaf, and longer ones from durable paper, *ce-saa*, produced from the insect-resistant bark of the Paper Mulberry or Saa tree (*Broussonetia papyrifera*).

In the 19th century, chests of various sizes were important items of Burmese furniture. Smaller ones were used for storing important domestic items, such as birth certificates and horoscopes, whilst larger ones were used to store bedding as well as manuscripts on religious instruction, important events and Buddhist teachings. Those found in monasteries were usually placed on stands, supported by four legs, and were often elaborately decorated with relief designs in gold leaf, lacquer and glass mosaic. The most common decorative themes were taken from the *Jataka*, stories about important events in the life of the Buddha.

These chests are made from teak (*Tectona hamiltoniana*), an endemic, tropical hardwood which is highly resistant to insect-attack. The wood is finished in lacquer, *yun*, produced from the sap of wild Burmese lacquer trees (*Gluta usitata*). The straw-coloured sap drains into tubes from cuts in the tree bark and, once oxygenated, turns a deep black colour. Panel designs are made in *thayo* clay relief. This process involves kneading wood or cow dung ashes with lacquer to form malleable strings. These are then sculpted or stamped into patterns on the finished lacquer surface. When each formed piece of *thayo* has hardened, it is lacquered and overlaid with 24-carat gold leaf. *Thayo* designs are often inset with mirror glass, as seen in this example on the far right of the main panel.

The stepped stand on which this chest sits suggests it came originally from a monastery rather than domestic abode. Monastery chests such as this held books recording Buddhist teaching and were placed at the focal point of monastery halls in Myanmar and Thailand. This fine example is raised on a four-legged, stepped stand in red lacquered wood and 24-carat gold leaf overlay. The stand's four feet represent Chinthei, the leonine guardian of Buddhism. The actual chest is elaborately decorated and beautifully preserved, with only minimal damage to the *thayo* relief. The scenes on the main panel illustrate scenes from the life of the Buddha, the main theme being 'the death of the Buddha'. It includes scenes of the Buddha surrounded by different types of worshippers and mourners including *pongyi* (Buddhist monks) and celestial beings. Three stickers on the back of the chest inform us that it was displayed in the Burmese Section of the 1924 British Empire Exhibition.

Emma Gilberthorpe, with thanks to Lewis Hill

Iban Headhunting Sword

30

Steel, brass, horn, rattan and human hair; Mandau length 66 cm, Scabbard 58 cm.

Sarawak
20th century CE

Gift from the Rt Hon Malcolm MacDonald
DUROM. 1976.119

Photograph of a dancing Iban warrior, by KF Wong.

20th century CE

Gift from the Rt Hon Malcolm MacDonald
DUROM. 1976.179.77

This *Mandau* (Iban) or *Parang Ilang* (Malay) sword belonged to Temenggong Koh anak Jubang (1870–1956). Traditionally the *mandau* is the prized headhunting weapon of the Dayak peoples of Borneo. This is a typical Iban example in good condition. The hilt is of horn, the grip bound with rattan, above a plain cast brass ferrule, into which the tang of the blade is firmly cemented with resin. A hank of human hair enhances the top of the pommel, while the horn prong below is elaborately carved in a 'leech' design with a tuft of dyed red hair at its tip. The gently curved steel blade has a single edge, with a chiselled decoration of two leaves below the tang. The back is almost straight for three-quarters of its length, where another chiselled design begins a curve down to the point. Characteristically, the blade in section is markedly convex on one side and slightly concave on the other, a feature said to improve its cutting ability.

The scabbard is made of two flat pieces of hardwood shaped to fit the blade and bound together with four decorative ties of braided rattan. The upper part is carved in high relief. On the back of the sheath is a plain bast pocket containing a knife (*munbat* [Iban] or *piso raout* [Malay]) with a small blade and long handle. The pocket is decorated with three hangings of black hair, with a white feather attached below by a string of red, white and green beads. At the top is a loop of braided rattan for suspending the sword from the waist.

In July 1946 Sarawak was ceded to the British Crown by the last White Rajah. Malcolm MacDonald was Governor-General of Malaya and British Borneo at the time, and he went to Kuching for the ceremony. Later on a tour of the interior he met Temenggong Koh, paramount chief of the Iban, whom he describes as the most important pagan in Sarawak. Koh was in his seventies but still active and powerful; only the previous year he had directed activities against the Japanese on the Rejang River, warfare that effectively marked the end of head-hunting in Sarawak.

Over the next few years they became good friends. Macdonald visited Koh's longhouse many times, and he got to know him and his family so well that Koh later adopted him as a son during a return visit to Malaya. This period is affectionately described and beautifully illustrated in Macdonald's book *Borneo People*.

Temenggong Koh was an Iban war leader who had risen to office under the White Rajahs as they brought the peoples of the Borneo interior under their rule and established the boundaries of Sarawak. He had achieved fame as the mightiest Iban head-hunter. Traditionally the taking of a head was marked by a tattoo on the back of one joint of one finger. Koh's hands were tattooed all over, and Macdonald believed that Koh had taken over a hundred heads with this *mandau*.

Lewis Hill

CAMBODIAN XYLOPHONE

31

Wood, textile; length 98cm, width 33cm

Kampuchea (Cambodia)
Early 20th century CE

Gift from Rt Hon Malcolm MacDonald
DUROM.1976.116

Cambodia's flamboyant royal figurehead, Norodom Sihanouk (born 1922) gave this musical instrument to Malcolm MacDonald at some point between 1948, when the two first met, and 1955, when Sihanouk abdicated the throne to rule as prime minister. This was a period of great change for Cambodia: after hundreds of years of existing as a vassal state to the Siamese and Vietnamese, and then as part of the French Indochinese Union, in 1953, King Sihanouk boldly declared the country's independence.

In his notes about the instrument, MacDonald recollects that it was from Sihanouk's own *Royal Corps de Ballet* – and the Royal crest can be seen prominently displayed on both ends. McDonald may even have heard this instrument being played, for he vividly

106

describes attending a performance by the Royal group in 1948 in his book *Angkor and the Khmers*. In any case, the instrument was probably manufactured at around that time, judging by its style and condition.

The art form that the *Royal Corps* performed, and which has long been patronised by the Khmer Court, is *pinpeat* – a form that has close parallels throughout South East Asia, including in neighbouring Thailand (*piphat*). The full *pinpeat* ensemble consists of two xylophones, two circular racks of gongs, a glockenspiel-type instrument, a pair of finger-cymbals, two drums, two oboes, and a group of singers. Performance has traditionally also incorporated court ceremony, dance-drama, masked theatre, or shadow puppet theatre, with narrative material mainly from the Khmer version of the Hindu Ramayana, the *Reamker*.

Following his mother's initiative, Sihanouk was highly committed to making *pinpeat* performance an important part of the Khmer Royal Court, and his daughter, Princess Norodom Bopha Devi, eventually became a leading dancer. It is not surprising that the Royals were keen to promote the form, for it can be traced back to the enormously powerful Khmer Empire, with scenes from the *Reamker* and *pinpeat*-like ensembles clearly depicted on the walls of Angkor Wat. Hence, MacDonald's own response to the 1948 performance:

'The story gave me a fascinating glimpse of the link between the past and the present, the unbroken history of the Khmer people…'

The *roneat ek* is the smaller of the two xylophones (*roneat*) used in *pinpeat* and, as its name suggests ('*ek*' meaning 'the first'), it acts as the leader of the ensemble. Because the performer's usual role is to weave rapid scales around the main melody with both hands playing in octaves, the instrument is sometimes also known as '*roneat rut*' ('running xylophone').

This particular instrument displays a typical construction. The boat-shaped sound box (just under a metre long) is made of a hardwood and sits on a raised square base. Between the leaf-shaped wooden upper ends, which recollect the leaves of the bodhi tree under which the Buddha attained enlightenment, 21 bamboo sound bars are strung along two cords. These are all the same width, but not the same length or thickness, as these dimensions determine the pitch of the bars. In accordance with Khmer musical theory, there are seven notes to the octave, with similar pitch intervals between each note (in contrast with the Western major scale) – giving a three-octave range. For fine tuning, musicians commonly apply round knobs of lead, beeswax, and rosin beneath the slabs and, on this instrument, residue still remains. The beaters, presented with the instrument, are also typical: bamboo sticks about 40cm long, with heads of tightly bound cloth.

Like Sihanouk himself, the *roneat ek* is the leader of an ancient Khmer institution and it is hard to imagine a more appropriate, symbolic gift. Also like Sihanouk, this particular instrument has proved a survivor; instruments predating the Khmer Rouge's reign (1975–1979), when people and things deemed 'bourgeois' were destroyed on a massive scale, are extremely rare.

Simon Mills

Wooden Panel Showing Scenes From The Ramayana

32

Hardwood; height 64cm, width 169cm

Indonesia, Bali
1987 CE

Gift from Dr JT Roberts
DUROM.1999.102

This carved wooden panel from the island of Bali shows scenes from the Ramayana, the ancient Hindu epic which tells the story of Prince Rama and his quest to save his beloved wife Sita after she is kidnapped by the demon King Ravana. Originating in India, it is thought that the Ramayana was first written down somewhere between 500–100 BCE.

The Ramayana traditionally includes 24,000 verses in seven *kandas* or books and was written in Sanskrit. Like India's other great epic, the Mahabharata, it is not just a good story, but a vehicle for the teachings of the ancient Hindu sages. These teachings are transmitted both through the use of allegory in the story, and through passages of a more obvious philosophical or devotional nature. The Ramayana is traditionally attributed to the sage Valmiki, who is viewed in the story as a contemporary of Rama and features as a character in the final book. The epic tale has had an enormous influence on literature and art beyond India itself, across the whole Indian subcontinent and South East Asia. Versions of the story exist in written and oral form in Thailand, Malaysia, Laos, Vietnam, Cambodia, Indonesia and the Maldives. The panel shown here was carved in Bali.

Prince Rama, the hero of the story, is portrayed as an incarnation of the god Vishnu and the epitome of virtue. Rama is the eldest and favourite son of Dasharatha, king of Kosala, the capital of which was the city of Ayodhya. The opening book deals with Rama's birth, childhood and marriage to the beautiful Sita (Sinta in Indonesian), portrayed as an incarnation of Lakshmi, consort of Vishnu. In the second book, the elderly king prepares to hand over his realm to Rama. However, in order to keep a promise to one of his wives, Kaikeyi, Dasharatha is forced to banish Rama into the wilderness and name her son, Bharata, as his successor.

Rama accepts his father's decree and is followed into exile by Sita and his younger brother and constant companion Lakshmana. Sita, Rama and Lakshmana are shown together on the left-hand side of the panel, standing in front of a temple.

The third book deals with the adventures of Rama, Sita and Lakshmana in the forest and the beginning of their struggle with Ravana. Ravana (Rawana in Indonesian) is a *rakshasa*, often translated as demon, and king of Lanka. He is aided in his plan to kidnap Sita by the *rakshasa* Maricha. Maricha disguises herself as a golden deer, shown to the right of centre on this panel. Sita is captivated by the beauty of the deer and urges Rama to capture it for her. Rama is suspicious but is unable to dissuade Sita and so goes into the forest in search of the deer, ordering Lakshmana to stay with Sita and keep her safe. But soon Sita hears what she thinks is Rama's voice calling for help and she insists that Lakshmana leave her to aid her husband. This is a further trick and once Lakshmana is gone, Ravana is able to kidnap Sita. Jatayu, a vulture, attempts to rescue Sita but is mortally wounded in the struggle and lives just long enough to tell Rama of the abduction. The kidnap of Sita forms the central image of our panel. Later books tell of Rama's alliance with Hanuman, one of the *vanara*, a race of ape-like people, and of their ultimately successful struggles to rescue Sita and to return Rama to his rightful throne.

The Oriental Museum is fortunate to own the Roberts Collection of Balinese art, a substantial collection of sculpture, woodcarving and paintings created in Bali during the later part of the 20th century. The collection charts the change from traditional polychrome painted woodcarving created for temples to pieces such as this one, created to serve a new international art market.

Rachel Grocke

NEAR AND MIDDLE EAST

The terms Near East and Middle East do not have precise definitions. Broadly speaking they are used to define the region where Africa, Europe and Asia meet. Today the boundaries of the region are generally taken to include Egypt, Jordan, Israel, Lebanon, Syria, Iraq, Iran and the countries of the Arabian Peninsula (Saudi Arabia, Yemen, Oman, United Arab Emirates, Qatar, Bahrain and Kuwait). At either end countries such as Libya, Turkey, Sudan and Afghanistan can also be included.

Standing at the crossroads between continents, this region has an enormously complex history. Despite having been the unhappy subject of seemingly endless waves of conquest and counter-conquest, it has benefited from its role at the centre of international trade and travel, and acted as a melting pot for knowledge, languages and cultures. Beginning with the rise of Sumer in the 4th millennium BCE, the region was one of the birthplaces of civilisation, as well as giving rise to the major religions of Judaism, Christianity and Islam.

The characters associated with the Oriental Museum's ancient Near Eastern collections read like a *Who's Who* of early 20th-century archaeology. Through his wide-ranging network of contacts Professor Thacker was able to secure collections for the museum from Sir Leonard Woolley's excavations at Ur; from Kathleen Kenyon's excavations at Jericho; from the excavations at Lachish sponsored by Henry Wellcome; and from a number of other sites. There is even a single brick dated to Nebuchadnezzar II, the Babylonian ruler mentioned in the biblical Book of Daniel, reputedly excavated by Lawrence of Arabia and passed by him to Gertrude Bell!

Thanks to Henry Percy, eldest son of the 7th Duke of Northumberland, the Northumberland Collection also includes a significant number of Near Eastern seals and tablets inscribed with the cuneiform script. In addition to the ancient material there is a small collection of objects dating to the Christian era including ceramics, metal crucifixes and tombstones.

The museum's collections from the Islamic Period are relatively small, but include fine examples of calligraphy and medieval and post-medieval ceramics as well as works in jade and bronze. Artefacts in this collection come mainly from Syria, Iran and Turkey.

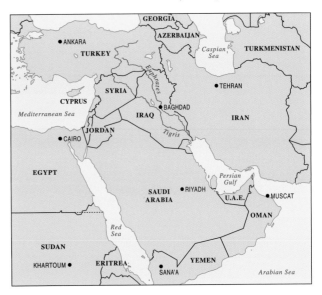

Left: Mina'i ware bowl (no. 36).

Barrel Cylinder of Nebuchadnezzar II

33

Fired clay; length 13.5cm, diameter 6.8cm

Iraq
Reign of Nebuchadnezzar II, 599 BCE

Northumberland Collection
DUROM.N2271

This barrel cylinder, which is one of the outstanding possessions of the Oriental Museum, is a beautifully preserved inscription of the Neo-Babylonian king Nebuchadnezzar II, of biblical fame. It commemorates his restoration of the Ebabbar in Sippar, the main temple of the sun-god Šamaš, and can be dated to 599 BCE, near the beginning of his reign. The cylinder was originally part of the collection of Henry Algernon George Percy, Earl Percy (1871–1909), and was purchased by Durham University in 1950. It came to the attention of the scholarly community when Berger described it in 1973. Until then, the text of the cylinder had been known from other copies in London and New York – but this inscription has unique features, revealing the individual craft of the scribe.

The Ebabbar inscription of Nebuchadnezzar II follows the tripartite structure that is typical of Neo-Babylonian royal inscriptions. It starts with the king introducing himself, then gives an account of his building work, and concludes with a prayer to the sun-god. The text's thematic unity depends in large part on the connections between Nebuchadnezzar as the 'king of justice' and Šamaš as the Mesopotamian god of justice. Stylistically, it is written in the literary idiom of the Neo-Babylonian royal inscriptions. A good example of the expressive range and sheer exuberance of its language can be found in the climactic central section of the text, when Nebuchadnezzar initiates his building work:

> *uqa"â Šašši, ašši qati, usappâ Šašši*
> '*I waited on Šamaš, I raised my hands (in prayer), I prayed to Šamaš*'.

The rare phonetic spelling ša-aš-ši (rather than expected dUTU) draws attention to a striking pun on the Sun god's name: Šašši, ašši… Šašši ('the Sun, I raised… the Sun'). Various other features such as assonance (uqa"â… qati, 'I waited on… my hands'), syntactical parallelism (uqa"â Šašši… usappâ Šašši), and phonetic chiasm (…Šašši, ašši…), make for a hymnic piece of literary prose. The passage as a whole evokes a momentous encounter between god and king.

Like other inscriptions of its kind, the Durham cylinder takes the form of a barrel made of fired clay. It may originally have been deposited in the walls of the Ebabbar, or it may have been kept as an archive copy in Sippar or elsewhere. All known copies of the Ebabbar cylinder, including this example, are arranged in three columns. However, the Durham inscription diverges from other known copies in that the text is spaced out unevenly across the columns, leaving too much text for column 3. Rather than assuming clumsiness on the part of an otherwise competent scribe, we might see this as a conscious attempt to create identifying tags around the empty spaces between columns: 'the temple of Shamash'–'which is in Sippar'–'his temple Ebabbar'–'which is in Sippar'. The effect is striking, and, if interpreted correctly, would make the Durham copy of the Ebabbar inscription an interesting example of Mesopotamian scribal practice.

Johannes Haubold

Carved Relief From the Palace of Ashurbanipal at Nineveh

34

Alabaster; length 71cm, height 43.5cm

Iraq, Kuyunjik
Reign of Ashurbanipal, 668–627 BCE

Transferred from Durham Castle
DUROM.1950.4

Archaeological remains from the site of Nineveh (today known as Kuyunjik) on the banks of the river Tigris, indicate that the area was first occupied in the 7th millennium BCE and that it remained an important site of human occupation until eclipsed by the city of Mosul on the opposite riverbank.

At the end of the 8th century BCE the Assyrian King Sennacherib (reigned 704–681 BCE) chose Nineveh as his capital and built what he called the 'Palace Without Rival', decorating it with finely carved reliefs. Nineveh made a natural site for a capital city. It lay in fertile, grain-producing land at an important river crossing site and contained the chief temple of the goddess Ishtar. In Sennacherib's time the city occupied more than 7 square kilometres and was surrounded by more than 12 kilometres of wall. As well as constructing palaces and other buildings the king undertook major irrigation works, creating orchards, fields and a royal park where rare plants were cultivated. These included the exotic 'wool-bearing tree' – cotton – imported from India.

At this time the Assyrians had carved an empire that stretched from Egypt to the Persian Gulf, but this empire was not easy to control and Sennacherib's successor Esarhaddon died in 669 BCE while on an expedition to crush rebellion in Egypt. Esarhaddon was succeeded by Ashurbanipal (reigned 668–627 BCE). Ashurbanipal was also a military leader and led further campaigns to regain control of Egypt for the Assyrian Empire. However, he was also proud to be a scholar. He could read and write both Akkadian and Sumerian and boasted of being able to solve complex mathematical problems. Perhaps his greatest legacy is the library that he created at Nineveh. He sent agents out across the empire to make copies of documents and return them to the library. It included works of literature, vocabularies and word lists, royal chronicles, medical treatises, ritual and magical texts. It is one of the greatest sources of knowledge that has survived to us from ancient Mesopotamia.

Ashurbanipal built a new palace, now known as the Northern Palace. This building housed the magnificent library and was also decorated with finely carved stone reliefs, including the famous lion hunt carvings now in the British Museum. The relief shown here is one of two sections now in the Oriental Museum that come from this palace. It depicts the results of civil war between Assyria and Babylon.

Prior to his death Esarhaddon had created a treaty that ensured that Ashurbanipal should succeed him as king of Assyria, while his brother Shamash-shum-ukin would assume the throne in Babylon. For many years this system of dual monarchy seems to have worked well, though it is clear that Ashurbanipal was the senior of the two. However in 652 BCE the brothers seem to have quarrelled, and for reasons that are not clear, civil war broke out. Eventually Ashurbanipal laid siege to Babylon itself. After two years the city finally fell, with Shamash-shum-ukin dying in his palace as it burned just before the city surrendered.

This relief shows an auxiliary solider in the Assyrian army, recognisable by his crested helmet, with Babylonian prisoners. It is thought to come from the Inner Court of Ashurbanipal's Palace, from a section that depicts vanquished southerners being deported to Assyria after the war had ended. The three male prisoners on the left are followed by an Assyrian soldier, who is using a stick to beat the captive in front of him. Behind them are three female prisoners. These can be identified as Babylonian by their distinctive fringed dresses and their hairstyles. On the far right-hand side is the figure of a boy turning towards a figure which has now been lost. As several of the women are carrying water skins he may be asking for a drink.

Rachel Grocke

Ceremonial Macehead

35

Blue marble; length 7cm, diameter 4.5cm

Iraq
7th century BCE

Northumberland Collection
DUROM.N2266

In Mesopotamia during the early millennia BCE a mace was a formidable weapon of war. A heavy piece of shaped stone mounted on a sturdy shaft, it could crush limbs and break bones in battle. A skilled warrior armed with such a weapon was a man to be respected and feared.

By the time this mace was made, in the 7th century BCE, advances in technology and warfare had made the mace more or less obsolete as a major weapon, but it still retained its aura of military power. In fact, carrying such a traditional shape and type of weapon symbolised more than mere superiority on the battlefield, it hinted at fathers and sons that had passed military prowess through generations of warriors from mighty ancestors that had used such maces in war themselves.

A further glance at this mace would tell you even more about its owner. The striking colour instantly lets you know that this is made of no ordinary stone but a dazzling blue marble. The piece of marble, while very beautiful, is not a suitable stone to be useful as a mace – indeed you can see the flaws in the piece that would fly apart if any serious attempt were made to use it as a weapon. So this is a mace for a man who wields military might, but has no need of personal defence; a weapon not for a common soldier but for a commander of armies.

But the use of blue marble tells the observer still more about the extent of the power held by the owner of the mace. This is not a common or cheap stone. The man who possessed this mace had the wealth and authority to have such a large and rare stone sought out, purchased and worked into his desired shape. He had the position and influence necessary among the merchants, traders and craftsmen required for such an operation, and to have it carved and polished with such fine assurance.

To add to this endorsement of the owner's civil position, the mace has two cuneiform inscriptions, one on either side, so no observer could fail to see at least one of them. Cuneiform is the earliest writing system known, and one that can be used to write several languages. But its use and understanding was restricted to a small, highly educated scribal class. Anyone who saw the inscriptions on this mace would know, without needing to read the inscriptions, that its owner was someone with power and influence among this elite, possibly even someone who could read the signs themselves.

The inscription is dedicated to Nabu-mukin-apli, 'for his own life, for the length of his days, for his happiness and for the security of his position'. It is a testament to the strength of the statement this mace makes about him and his authority, both civil and military, that we can still know so much of his aspirations in society more than two and a half thousand years later.

Helen Armstrong

36

MINA'I WARE BOWL

Fritware; diameter 22cm

Iran
Seljuq-Ilkhan Dynasty, 1100–1299 CE

The Art Fund
DUROM.1983.21

This piece is a splendid example of Mina'i pottery, an Islamic ceramic tradition that is distinct in both style and technology. While the other examples of Islamic glazed pottery in the museum's collection provide valuable insight into this elite craft industry, this object in particular is a treasure due to both the uniqueness of the Mina'i tradition, and the finesse of the artist responsible for the decorative motifs we see on the bowl. Mina'i pottery may be described simply as a polychrome enamelled ware. The tradition developed in Kashan, Persia, during the 12th century CE, but was fading out by the 14th century CE. As such, Mina'i pottery can be seen as an elite industry unique to the Seljuq Dynasty. This dynasty was known for reinvigorating Islamic crafts, and Mina'i pottery is just one example of the artistic innovation taking place in Persia during that time.

This particular bowl shows two figures facing one another on horseback. The facial expressions of the two men and their horses are quite remarkable. Also seen on the bowl is a tree flanked by two pheasant-like birds between the figures. Surrounding this scene are motifs widely used on Islamic glazed pottery, and include the half-circle decoration around the rim. An inscription in Kufic is seen running around the interior of the bowl just below the half-circles, and a second calligraphic motif adorns the exterior surface of the bowl. Previous descriptions of this Mina'i bowl highlight this inscription as being 'imitation'. Indeed, pseudo-calligraphy is known to have been used on elite Islamic pottery of this period, and is a testament to the beauty of the written script. The motifs seen on this bowl are exquisitely executed in polychrome decoration. The decoration on Mina'i pottery often shows complex scenes, displaying a number of figures and actions, with examples of bowls depicting hunting scenes and Persian legends. In this sense, Mina'i decoration is reflective of the designs found in contemporary manuscript illustrations, rather than a continuation of earlier ceramic decorative traditions. The common practice of depicting human and animal figures on Mina'i pottery is also quite distinct in Islamic art in general, due to this practice being expressly forbidden in the *Hadith*, a collection of oral traditions on the words and actions of the Prophet.

The process of manufacturing Mina'i ware was described by Abu'l-Qasim in his *Treatise on Ceramics*, part of a larger manuscript first published in 1301 CE and describing, in detail, the various Persian craft industries. The complexity of the manufacturing process of this elite pottery was thoroughly outlined, from the procurement of the clay and stone used to make the body of the bowls, to the highly controlled firing processes. The application of the colourants was a key step in the making of Mina'i pottery. Those pigments used to create blue and turquoise are more stable, and were applied before the glaze was fired. The less-stable colours – namely red, black, white, and gold – were applied onto the cooled glaze following this firing. The bowl then needed to be fired again to fix these colourants to the glaze, with the kiln held at a different temperature than that of the first firing. Thus, while this bowl is indeed beautiful in its own right, understanding the complexities and the skill that went into its creation allow us to see it as a superb example of the heights of Islamic art.

Robert Cumming

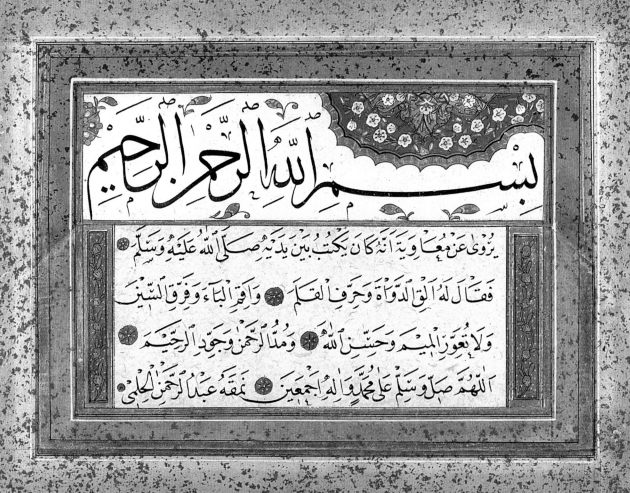

بِسْمِ اللهِ الرَّحْمٰنِ الرَّحِيمِ

يُرْوَى عَنْ مُعَاوِيَةَ اَنَّهُ كَانَ يَكْتُبُ بَيْنَ يَدَيْهِ صَلَّى اللهُ عَلَيْهِ وَسَلَّمَ

فَقَالَ لَهُ اَلْقِ الدَّوَاةَ وَحَرِّفِ الْقَلَمَ ۞ وَاَقِمِ الْبَاءَ وَفَرِّقِ السِّينَ

وَلَا تُعَوِّرِ الْمِيمَ وَحَسِّنِ اللهَ ۞ وَمُدَّ الرَّحْمٰنَ وَجَوِّدِ الرَّحِيمَ ۞

اَللّٰهُمَّ صَلِّ وَسَلِّمْ عَلٰى مُحَمَّدٍ وَآلِهِ اَجْمَعِينَ ۞ نَمَقَهُ عَبْدُ الرَّحْمٰنِ الْحِلْمِي

37

ISLAMIC CALLIGRAPHY

Paper; height 9cm, width 14cm

Ottoman Empire
17th century CE

Purchased
DUROM.1983.1

Writing is a practical means of imparting knowledge, but it also stands at the very heart of Islamic art. In the Islamic world calligraphy – the practice of artistic handwriting – has deep religious roots and harnesses the power of the written word in both Arabic and Persian. Since it was traditionally the primary medium for the preservation of the Qur'an, calligraphy came to be the most revered of the Islamic arts. That notwithstanding, this most Islamic of all the Muslim arts has its figurative sides as well, and calligraphers can create works of great beauty by the skillful interweaving of written words and letters or through the inspired use of micrography.

Calligraphy has arguably become the most venerated form of Islamic art because it provides a direct link between the languages of the world's Muslims and the religion of Islam. The Qur'an has played a central role in the development and evolution of the Arabic language and, by extension, Arabic calligraphy. Proverbs and complete passages from the Qur'an still provide potently inspirational sources for Islamic calligraphers. Such calligraphers can draw upon the 28 letters of the Arabic alphabet and employ no fewer than 18 different forms of writing. Furthermore, Persian art and civilization has been effective in creating the artistic form of design in Islamic calligraphy. The most common script for everyday use is *Ruq'ah* (also known as *Riq'a*). The Persian form of writing is called *Nastaliq*. Simple and easy to write, its movements are small, and controlled. It is considered to be superior to *Naskh* script, which children are taught first. The traditional instrument of the Arabic calligrapher is the *qalam*, a pen made of dried reed or bamboo; the ink used is often coloured, and selected so that its intensity can vary greatly, ensuring that the bolder strokes of the compositions are very dynamic in their effect.

Other media using calligraphy included coins and textiles. Beginning in 692 CE the Islamic caliphate reformed the coinage of the Near East by replacing visual depiction with words. This was especially true for dinars, or gold coins of high value, which were generally inscribed with quotes from the Qur'an. During the 10th century CE, the Persians began weaving inscriptions onto elaborately patterned silks. So highly treasured were these textiles that Crusaders brought them to Europe as prized possessions.

One of Islam's greatest calligraphers was Ibn Muqla (886–940 CE). He developed the geometric principles used by his successors to keep letters in proportion, and he also helped develop the cursive script known as *Naskh*. There were many different script styles, which differed in various centuries and throughout the widespread regions of the Islamic world. Perhaps the finest example of Islamic calligraphy to be found in the Oriental Museum's collection is a 17th-century decorative panel produced by the Ottoman artist, Abd al-Rahman al-Hilmi. Written in *thuluth* and *naskhi* scripts, the panel is headed by the Bismillah, 'In the name of Allah, the Compassionate, the Merciful', below which is reproduced the Prophet's instructions on how it should be written:

'It is related concerning Mu'awiyah (the first Umayad caliph) that he was writing in the presence of the Prophet, may God bless him and grant him salvation! He said to him, "Set forth the inkwell and incline the pen. Straighten the ba and separate (the teeth of) the shin; do not mar the mim and embellish (the word) Allah. Extend the word al-Rahman (Compassionate) and make an excellent al-Rahim (Merciful). May God bless and grant salvation to Muhammad and the God of all. Written down by Abd al-Rahman al-Hilmi.'

Nowadays – as the rise of Islamic awareness is felt among contemporary Muslim peoples and a new sense of ethnic, national, and religious identity moves the people of the Third World – Muslim calligraphers are again exploring and experimenting with their art. An increased interest in calligraphy is evident today among Muslim patrons as well as artists in all parts of the Muslim world.

Javad Nateghpour

ANCIENT EGYPT

There are almost 7,000 objects in the Oriental Museum's Ancient Egyptian collections, ranging in date from the Pre-Dynastic (5500–3100 BCE) to the Coptic periods (after 395 CE) and covering almost all categories of object from monumental sculpture to woven sandals.

The core of the collection was formed by Algernon Percy, the Fourth Duke of Northumberland (1792–1865) in the mid-19th century. The Duke had developed a fascination for Egypt following his visit to the country in 1826 and in later years he developed large collections of both British and Egyptian antiquities, which he proudly displayed at the family seat of Alnwick Castle.

The Duke's collection of over 2,500 objects was largely purchased via English auctions rather than during his travels in Egypt and included material originally acquired by James Burton and by the British Consul, Henry Salt. It was fully published in 1880 in a lavish volume written by Samuel Birch and illustrated by Joseph Bonomi and it remained on display at Alnwick well into the 20th century, prior to being removed to the British Museum for conservation shortly before the outbreak of the Second World War.

In the 1940s the decision was taken to sell the collection. Both the British Museum and the Brooklyn Museum expressed an interest in acquiring all or part of the collection, but the Duke's successors were keen that it should remain intact and – if possible – in the North East of England. Happily, Durham University had also indicated its desire to obtain the collection and, thanks to the generous assistance of Dr and Mrs HN Spalding, was able to raise the asking price.

The scope of the collection reflects the Duke of Northumberland's particular academic interests. With Egyptology still in its infancy he was aware of the need to collect accurate copies of inscriptions that would further understanding of the hieroglyphic script and the ancient Egyptian language. His collection accordingly contained numerous inscribed stelae from all periods and other smaller items showing the language and script at different stages of development. The Duke's interest in establishing a chronology of Egypt is likewise reflected in the high number of pieces bearing royal names.

In 1971 the University's holdings of Egyptian artefacts were substantially enlarged by the acquisition of part of the collection of Sir Henry Wellcome. Wellcome, a founding partner of the well-known drug company, amassed one of the largest private collections ever made in the fields of archaeology, anthropology and the history of human health. After his death in 1936, it took more than 50 years for his Trustees to distribute the collection among museums and libraries across the UK. The Oriental Museum was fortunate to receive a collection of around 4,000 Egyptian artefacts. This material greatly strengthened the museum's holdings of amulets, stone tools and other Pre-Dynastic objects.

These two core collections have been supplemented by targeted purchases, other small donations and material from the archaeological excavations at Qasr Ibrim, Buhen and Saqqara carried out by WB Emery and the Egypt Exploration Society in the 1950s and 1960s with the support of Durham University.

The importance of the collections was recognised in 2008 when they received Designated Status from the Museums, Libraries and Archives Council as being of national and international importance.

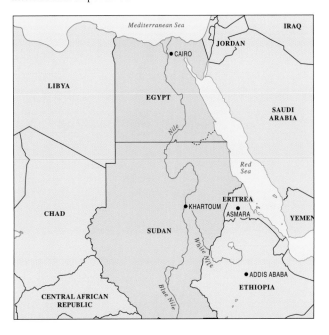

Left: bronze cat mummy case (no. 49).

38

Heb-sed Vessel of Pepi II

Calcite; height 16.5cm, diameter 15cm

Egypt
Old Kingdom, 6th Dynasty, about 2200 BCE

Northumberland Collection
EG4395

The doctrine of divine kingship lay at the heart of ancient Egyptian civilisation. It inspired the creation of dazzling monuments – pyramids and temples – and coloured all aspects of pharaonic religion and government. So it is not surprising that rituals to ensure the king's continued potency played an important part in the life of the court.

After the coronation, when the monarch first assumed the mantle of divinity, the most significant ceremony was the royal jubilee (*heb-sed* in ancient Egyptian). It was usually staged on the thirtieth anniversary of the king's accession and thereafter at shorter intervals. At its core, the *heb-sed* was a ritual of renewal, its various rites designed to rejuvenate the monarch and re-confirm his right to rule. The *heb-sed* was a symbolically-charged occasion, exploited to the full for propaganda purposes.

The *heb-sed* vase of Pepi II is a fine example of the objects commmissioned by ancient Egyptian rulers to celebrate their jubilees. It was probably produced in the royal workshops where the best craftsmen manufactured objects from the finest materials to celebrate the king. The vessel displays a simplicity and elegance of form typical of the Old Kingdom or Pyramid Age (the 26th to 22nd centuries BCE), the first great flowering of ancient Egyptian civilisation.

In form and decoration, the vase is replete with symbolism. Carved from a block of calcite (commonly called 'Egyptian alabaster'), its golden colour recalls the sun while its thin walls give it a magical translucence. The inscription on the front of the vessel, originally filled with pigment, concisely summarises the doctrine of divine kingship and the purpose of the *heb-sed*. A rectangular panel is formed by the signs for 'sky' (at the top), 'land' (at the bottom), and 'dominion' (to the left and right), symbolising the king's authority over all creation. The first column of text, giving the 'Horus-name' of Pepi II, expresses the fundamental tenet of ancient Egyptian kingship, namely that the king was the earthly incarnation of the sky-god Horus, represented as a falcon. In the second column, Pepi II's throne-name conveys the notion that the king embodied and reconciled the pairs of opposites that characterised the ancient Egyptians' world-view: Valley and Delta, floodplain and desert, etc. The third column records that the vessel was made 'on the first occasion of the *heb-sed*', while a horizontal band of hieroglyphs asserts that Pepi II has been 'made to live forever' – the central purpose of the jubilee festival.

Although pilloried in later folk-tradition for alleged weakness and licentiousness, Pepi II is famous chiefly for his longevity. The evidence suggests that he came to the throne at the age of six (in about 2265 BCE) and lived to be a centenarian, giving him a record-breaking reign of 94 years. By the standards of his time, and to most of his subjects, he must have seemed immortal. His jubilee and the vase produced to commemorate it had done their jobs well.

Toby Wilkinson

39

Stela of Dedu

Limestone; height 115cm, width 70cm

Egypt
Middle Kingdom, 12th Dynasty, 13th year of Senwosret I, 1944 BCE

Northumberland Collection
EG503

During the Middle Kingdom (2055–1650 BCE), thousands of stelae were set up at Abydos in Middle Egypt, the cult centre of first Khenty-imentyw and then Osiris, who was believed to be buried in the tomb of the First Dynasty king, Djer, on the Umm el-Qa'ab. Many of the stelae are commemorative rather than funerary, with excavation and research at the site revealing that the majority of the stelae were not connected with burials. The stelae from Abydos are associated with a change in Afterlife beliefs that occurred after the end of the Old Kingdom (2686–2181 BCE), often referred to as the 'democratisation of the Afterlife', where non-royal individuals could assume the previously royal prerogative of the role of Osiris in the Afterlife. Attendance at the Osiris festivals celebrated at Abydos became essential in order to guarantee access to the Osirian Afterlife, and simultaneously displayed an individual's social status, which was closely connected with levels of participation in the festivals. Stelae such as that of Dedu allowed the dedicator to partake, in absentia and for eternity, in the Osiris festivals.

The stela of the Steward, Dedu, dated to year 13 of the 12th Dynasty ruler, Senwosret I (reigned 1965–1920 BCE), is an impressive example of an Abydos stela. The upper section consists of a finely-cut sunk relief inscription which begins with the standard Offering Formula addressed to Osiris, Wepwawet, Hekat, Khnum and all the gods of Abydos, securing sustenance for Dedu in the Afterlife. This is followed by the Call to the Living requesting that those who read the inscription remember Dedu in the Osiris temple and during the festivals, including the well-known First Procession and Great Procession, as well as ensuring that Dedu actively participates in the festivals. The lower section depicts, in raised relief, a large figure of Dedu seated on the left with a dog beneath his chair. He is formally dressed in a broad collar and kilt, and holds a hand to his chest in a gesture of respect. Above him is a table of cosmetics, including a mirror in a case, an object with symbolic associations of regeneration in the Afterlife.

On the left are three registers of smaller figures, members of Dedu's family, whose names, originally indicated in paint, are now lost. The family members are portrayed bringing offerings that include a duck and an ox leg, these being further symbols of magical regeneration and strength. The only individuals who can be identified are Ren-iker, Dedu's brother, who stands on the top register below his name in the inscription, together with his wife, and Dedu's wife, who is seated before an offering table in the lower register.

The whole of the stela would have been painted – some darkened green paint remains on the flowers and vegetables – creating a striking monument when first installed. The stela acts as a record of Dedu's participation in the festivals at Abydos, presented in formal conventional terms that belie the social significance and emotional impact of the Osiris festivals and beliefs during the Egyptian Middle Kingdom.

Karen Exell

TRUSSED AND PLUCKED DUCK VESSEL

40

Blue anhydrite, copper rims for inlaid eyes; length 12cm, width 7cm, height 6.9cm

Egypt
Middle Kingdom, 13th Dynasty, about 1700 BCE

Gift of Sir Charles Edmund Hardinge
EG610

This strange and desirable object is a vessel, carefully carved in the form of a dead duck, with its neck and head lying on the breast and the wings and feet tightly folded against the body. The duck has been plucked as there are no feathers shown and the controlled character of the limbs suggests that they may have been bound. The pale blue stone used to make the duck vessel is blue anhydrite, which was especially admired by the Egyptians for its colour, waxy texture and ability to take detail and high polish. It is thought that a vein of the stone was discovered during the Middle Kingdom, but the precise location of the quarry has not been identified. A series of cosmetic vessels was made from the stone from Dynasty 12 to 13 (around 1900 to 1780 BCE) and then no more, presumably because the source had been mined out. The eye of the duck was once inlaid in another material within tiny copper rims. The skill of the craftsmen who made this object can be seen in the space carved out underneath the neck of the duck.

The duck vessel can only sit properly on its back, suggesting that it was used to hold a solid substance, which would not run out of the jar. There once may have been a lid or stopper for the jar, now lost, to ensure that the contents did not escape. The inside of the jar is itself narrow and rather tube-like, so that the whole of the inside of the duck was not carved out. Such tube-like containers were often used in Egypt as cosmetic holders, in particular for eye-paints such as green malachite or black kohl. The powdered pigments may have been mixed with water or with fat derived from duck or goose grease. They could then have been applied with an applicator, perhaps part of the stopper, designed to reach the bottom of the vessel.

The offering of a trussed duck was an important sign of access to elite foodstuffs as well as symbolic of the control of the wild forces of nature. In such a case the image of something dead and prepared for consumption did not have negative connotations. In addition, the light blue colour of the vessel evoked feelings of calmness and happiness, perhaps the result of make-up application. In any case, the size, quality and material of the jar suggest that it belonged to a person of the high elite, perhaps even from the family of the king himself. The closest parallel comes from a tomb at Abydos, dated to Dynasty 17, about 1700 BCE suggesting that such vessels were prized possessions, perhaps being passed down as heirlooms and eventually buried as part of the equipment for the Afterlife.

Penny Wilson

131

41

Funerary Mask

Gilded and painted cartonnage; height 45cm, width 33cm

Egypt
New Kingdom, 18th Dynasty, about 1500 BCE

Wellcome Collection
EG733

This fine mask was originally part of the Egyptian segment of the collection of the chemist and philanthropist Sir Henry Wellcome (1853–1936). This had been presented in 1964 by his trustees to the Petrie Museum of Egyptian Archaeology at University College London, and was then further distributed to other institutions around the United Kingdom, including the Oriental Museum. Like the vast majority of Wellcome's collection, the mask was certainly purchased on the antiquities market. However, it most probably originally came from the great necropolis of Western Thebes, opposite modern Luxor, ripped from the head of a mummy by local tomb-robbers in the late 19th or early 20th century CE.

The mask is made of cartonnage, a combination of plaster and linen that was a common material for the manufacture of masks and other items of mummy-adornment, and decorated with gold foil and paint. The latter had been applied directly to the finished, plastered, surface of the cartonnage, without any additional ground preparation. It shows the deceased wearing a so-called 'tripartite' wig in greenish-blue with gold striping, with an eleven-row collar in red, black and blue, edged with gilded drop-pendants.

These basic features and colours are common among Egyptian anthropoid coffins and masks of the early New Kingdom, i.e. the last years of the 16th and the first decades of the 15th centuries BCE. Thus, despite a lack of direct dating evidence, the mask can be attributed stylistically to somewhere around 1500 BCE. This is when Egypt's imperial ambitions were first manifested in Thutmose I's campaigns into northern Syria that extended Egyptian hegemony as far as the river Euphrates, and laid the foundations for Thutmose III's campaigns beyond that boundary a few decades later.

The gilded face, with the eyes picked out in paint, appears strangely out of proportion when compared with the rest of the mask. This seems to be a residual feature inherited from a group of curious mummy-masks made during the century or so prior to the manufacture of the Durham mask. These earlier masks combined a tiny face with the painted body, wings and legs of a vulture to apparently encase the head of the mummy with an image of the human-headed *ba-bird*, one of the manifestations of the human spirit. This concept was linked with the contemporary *rishi* (Arabic: 'feathered') anthropoid coffins, which seem to have been intended to show the whole mummy as a giant *ba*. The pure form of the 'rishi-masks' was short-lived, with the avian features withering to simply stylised wings and then disappearing altogether. However, the small size of face that formed part of the original conception lingered for some time afterwards, giving rise to such pieces as the Durham mask.

The mask and the mummy it once adorned will have been enclosed in a coffin, most probably of anthropoid shape, although examples of the old rectangular form were still to be found at the same time. Three variants of the anthropoid coffin existed around the time our mask was made, the aforementioned *rishi*, one painted to resemble a masked mummy enclosed in a white shroud (the 'white' coffin) and another which was primarily black – the Egyptian colour of resurrection.

Regardless of its exact provenance, the Durham mask is a fine example of Egyptian funerary art at the dawn of the country's imperial era, when Egypt would rule a territory that stretched from northern Syria to deep in Sudan.

Aidan Dodson

42

JAR INSCRIBED FOR QUEEN HATSHEPSUT

Travertine; height 21.7cm, diameter 20.7cm

Egypt
New Kingdom, 18th Dynasty, reign of Tuthmosis II, about 1485 BCE

Northumberland Collection
EG4402

Hatshepsut is best known as the regent queen who, ruling for her infant nephew Tuthmosis III, decided to assume full pharaonic powers for herself, ostensibly as the senior partner in a co-pharaohship with the young boy. In this role she prevailed in Egypt for more than twenty years, during which time her junior partner was maturing into the man who would go on to rule for thirty years after her death.

The large travertine jar on display in the museum, however, bears an inscription identifying it as part of the cosmetic equipment, not of King Hatshepsut, but of Hatshepsut the chief queen of her half-brother Tuthmosis II. In this role she is shown on several surviving stelae and monuments in the traditional queenly position behind her husband, who would himself sire his successor by a secondary wife.

Queen Hatshepsut and Tuthmosis II produced a daughter, Neferura, who was to be later so much part of Pharaoh Hatshepsut's plans for the future. The current scholarly opinion is that Neferura was their only daughter. It is, however, interesting to note that, in his autobiography, the old soldier, Ahmose Pennekheb, speaks of Neferura as their elder daughter.

This jar and its inscription brings into sharp focus the contrast between the realities of Hatshepsut's status and functions as queen, as evident in the historical record, and the extravagant claims which Pharaoh Hatshepsut was later to make in her inscriptions at her great funerary temple at Deir el-Bahri regarding her supposed status and ambitions during and after the reign of her father Tuthmosis I.

There she claims to have been sired by none other than great Amun himself in the form of her father in embrace with her mother.

She further asserts that it was she that her father had chosen as his true heir and that he had proclaimed her title during a royal progress with her among the great and good of Egypt. In the same vein some scholars have proposed that Hatshepsut intended to continue the female kingship in the person of her daughter, to whom she passed the sacred office of God's Wife. There is no evidence that Neferura married the young Tuthmosis III as would traditionally have happened. Whatever her gynocratic ambitions, they were thwarted by Neferura's early death whilst still in her teens.

The period of Hatshepsut's life indicated by the jar was also a time which brought into prominence a man of relatively humble origins who was to loom large as the *eminence grise* of Hatshepsut's reign. The wily and ambitious Senenmut began his association with the royal family as nurse-tutor to the infant Neferura. His closeness and intimacy with his charge and her mother is clear from the many statues he had made of himself holding close the young Neferura. It may well have been the death of Neferura which later precipitated his fall from grace.

Thus, this vessel may conjure for its observer a vision of the whole drama and daring of Hatshepsut's career in its contrasting phases. It is tempting to think that the fragrant contents of this jar may once have been rubbed into the skin of one of the most fascinating and powerful women of Ancient Egypt. It is thought that it later became a gift from the royal stores for the funerary equipment of a favoured official, perhaps the great Senenmut himself.

Ralph Austin

43

Shabti of Prince Bahmery

Sycamore wood; height 32.5cm

Egypt
New Kingdom, 18th Dynasty, about 1450 BCE

Northumberland Collection
EG517

In about 2000 BCE, when Egypt was ruled by the kings of the 11th Dynasty, the custom of placing mummiform statuettes of the deceased in the tomb made its appearance. They remained set items of the funerary equipment up to and including the reign of Queen Cleopatra, the last ruler of the Ptolemaic Dynasty, about 50 BCE. These statuettes were not only images of their deceased owner himself but were also intended to function on his behalf as a servant should he be called upon to do compulsory work in the Hereafter. Everybody, from exalted (even the King was not excluded) to lowly, male and female, had to perform corvées for the ruler of the Beyond, the god Osiris. Most statuettes have the form of a mummy in bandages, like the mummified body of the god Osiris. The Egyptians called such figurines *shabtis*. The origin of the name goes back to the word *shebed*, 'wooden stick'. In fact some of the earliest *shabtis* are roughly carved pieces of a tree branch. Later, from about 800 BCE, such figurines are commonly named *ushebti*, 'answerer', referring to their obligation to answer in the place of their masters ('present, here I am') when the names of the latter are called by the foreman of the work.

Shabtis are made of wax, wood, stone, terracotta or bronze. Some are veritable works of art like the wooden *shabti* shown here. Its size is impressive and the modelling and decoration are exquisite, as is the style of the hieroglyphs which adorn it. All details and the inscription are painted on a very thin layer of gesso. The deceased Prince Bahmery for whom the shabti was prepared is shown mummified, with a blue striated lappet wig. The face was originally adorned with a beard, now missing, fixed in a hole in the chin. The hands are not visible, which is typical for the earlier types of *shabti* figure. The front is inscribed with a 10-line hieroglyphic text containing a version of the *shabti* spell, Book of the Dead, chapter 6. It reads:

'The illuminated one, the King's Son Bahmery, he speaks: O, you shabtis, if the King's Son Bahmery is counted and called upon to do all the works which are wont to be done there [in the Netherworld], yes, an irritating obstacle is put in his way therewith – like a man at his duties at any time – namely to plough the fields, to irrigate the riparian lands and to transport sand by boat from east to west and vice versa, yes indeed 'Here I am, I shall do it', you shall say yonder.'

Who was the King's Son Bahmery? It seems that his *shabti* is the only source we have of this enigmatic prince. From the style of the figurine one may infer that it was produced during the first half of the 18th Dynasty, most probably in the time of Pharaoh Amenophis II, the seventh king of that dynasty. We know that Amenophis fathered at least ten sons, not all of whom are known by name. Presumably Prince Bahmery (a name meaning 'Beloved of the Inundation', or 'Beloved of the Morning Star'), the owner of one of the finest Egyptian treasures in Durham, was also a son of the famous Amenophis II.

Hans Schneider

44

BASKET WITH LID

Plant fibres; height 11cm, width 22.7cm

Egypt
18th Dynasty or later, after about 1450 BCE

Northumberland Collection
EG4968

Consider the number of plastic or cardboard containers you have in your home or workplace. It has been suggested that if we look at the number of these containers in our lives today we can gain a better idea of the importance of basketry in ancient societies. This was particularly the case in Ancient Egypt where wood was scarce but the raw materials for basket-making were to be found in abundance.

The Ancient Egyptians used a huge range of baskets, from small disposable bags to large decorated storage chests for clothes, bedding and the like. Rope could be made from tall, strong grasses (eg *Desmostachya bipinnata* and *Imperata cylindrica*) or from the rind of the papyrus stem (*Cyperus papyrus*). Baskets were made from dom palm leaves (*Hyphaena thebaica*) and, particularly from the Late Period onwards, date palm (*Phoenix dactylifera*). In the Ptolemaic Period rushes (*Juncus species*) also became a popular material both for baskets and mats.

The basket shown was made using the coil method. The first element, the bundle or foundation, is coiled and then held in place by a second element, the winder. This was one of the most popular basketry techniques during earlier periods of Egyptian history, together with twining and weaving. During the Ptolemaic and Roman periods other methods, such as plaiting, came into use. Baskets are still made today in Egypt from date palm leaves, while ropes and mats are created from the coarse fibres at the base of the leaves. Ethnoarchaeological studies of modern basket-making can provide a great deal of supplementary information on the processes of manufacture.

Given the importance that basketry had in Ancient Egypt, it might come as a surprise that very little has survived, transforming a basket such as the one shown here from an everyday object into one of the museum's treasures. There are several reasons for this. Perhaps the most obvious is that basketry was so commonplace that it tended to get overlooked. Indeed, many Ancient Egyptians discarding broken or worn out basketry may have burned it as fuel, thus removing all traces from the archaeological record. Furthermore, discarded basketry would also have been highly susceptible to destruction by insects, water and other causes of decay. More durable materials, such as pottery and stone are far more resilient and accordingly much more likely to survive through the centuries.

Basketry is most likely to have survived when placed in the dry, sealed environment of a desert tomb. However, early archaeologists in search of treasures to take back to the grand museums of the West during the 19th century did not care much for humble baskets and it is likely that many examples were simply discarded as being of little interest.

We are very lucky that Lord Prudhoe acquired such a fine example, probably from a New Kingdom tomb. It contains pieces of linen, although we cannot be sure if these are the original contents or were added later by an enterprising antiquities dealer. Whatever the case, this humble everyday object is now one of the museum's most precious objects. Indeed, among almost 7,000 objects in the Egyptian collections at the Oriental Museum, this is one of only two baskets.

Rachel Grocke

45

SPHINX OF TUTHMOSIS IV

Diorite; height 19.5cm, length 28.5cm, width 9.5cm

Egypt
New Kingdom, 18th Dynasty, about 1400 BCE

Northumberland Collection
EG3997

The sphinx is one of the most instantly recognisable of Ancient Egyptian symbols. The Great Sphinx at Giza was the largest statue ever made in Ancient Egypt, or indeed in the whole ancient world, and many other smaller examples survive from a variety of contexts. It has even been suggested that the word sphinx comes from the Ancient Egyptian phrase *shesep-ankh,* meaning 'living image' – a term occasionally used in reference to sphinxes.

The Ancient Egyptian sphinx usually has the head of a man and the body of a lion and was seen as benevolent, in contrast to Greek sphinxes which are more often female and often malicious. In Ancient Egypt the lion was associated with protection and defence. Images of lions were placed on door-bolts to enhance their protective function and lion-headed gargoyles are found on the waterspouts on Egyptian temple roofs, subduing the power of the rain. Royal thrones and beds often incorporate lion motifs as a talisman against harm.

Lions also have strong solar associations. The god Aker was a lion deity who guarded the gates of the horizon through which the sun passed into and out of the sky each day. The god Horus could also be depicted in leonine form as Horemakhet and was associated with the rising sun. It is not clear how early in Egyptian history this association was made but it may be that the Great Sphinx at Giza is both guardian of the necropolis and a representation of the king as the sun god.

The Oriental Museum's sphinx bears the cartouche of King Tuthmosis IV (1419–1386 BCE) and can be understood as a depiction of this king wearing the *nemes* headdress, which resembles a lion's mane. The guardian role of the sphinx meant it was often used at gates or doorways, or to line avenues leading to tomb or temple entrances. This sphinx was probably originally one of a pair or series of such guardians.

The insciption around the base of the statue, however, dates from around 100 years after Tuthmosis IV and belongs to the '*royal scribe and scribe of recruits, Ronero*'. From this we can deduce that the sphinx had somehow passed from its original function into the ownership of this scribe. The inscription is a funerary offering formula so we can assume that the sphinx was reused as part of Ronero's burial.

Indeed, its story does not end there. After the statue was purchased by the Duke of Northumberland in the 19th century it was used as the model for the pair of bronze sphinxes which now flank the obelisk known as Cleopatra's Needle, on the Embankment in London. There is also evidence to suggest that this image then served as the model for one of the versions of the sphinx which featured as bonnet ornaments on Armstrong Siddeley cars during the early 20th century.

It is interesting to note that in the 19th century the cartouche on the sphinx was misread as belonging to Tuthmosis IV's predecessor, Tuthmosis III. Hence it is the name of Tuthmosis III – *mn-hpr-re* – that appears on the chest of the sphinx on the Embankment rather than that of Tuthmosis IV – *mn-hprw-re*.

Rachel Grocke

Detail of the cartouche of Tuthmosis IV on the chest of the sphinx.

DECORATED BOXES OF PERPAUTY AND HIS WIFE ADY

46

Sycamore wood; height 44cm, width 51.5cm

Egypt
New Kingdom, 18th Dynasty, about 1370 BCE

Northumberland Collection
EG4572

Unlike the cedars of Lebanon and the hardwoods of Africa the principal trees of Egypt, the date palms, acacia and sycamore, produce poor timber for woodworkers; but happily the same dry climate that discourages the growth of trees is responsible for the preservation of many fine examples of the woodworker's craft. Working with such poor material and with basic bronze tools the Ancient Egyptian carpenters nevertheless turned out work of high quality that was both practical and aesthetically pleasing.

This magnificent box is the finer of two in the museum belonging to a man whose name is written in more than one way on each box but which we may read as Perpau or Perpauty. He claims no important title although he must have been a man of some means and station to have such fine funeral equipment. On one of the long sides of this box he is shown with his wife, Ady, receiving gifts from a son and three daughters in a typical Egyptian funerary scene. On the other side Perpauty is seated alone, receiving gifts from another son and two daughters, one of whom is already known from the first side. On this second side however, Perpauty and his son are shown unusually in silhouette, giving the decoration a sombre tone and perhaps attempting to portray the figures as lifeless. On each gable end of the box is a stylised tree with a pair of goats reaching up to graze on

the foliage, a rare motif in Egypt but better known in Near Eastern art.

The box is made of sycamore wood and is fitted with an intricate locking device with a latch that dropped into place after the lid was in position so that once closed it could not be opened without using force. It was most probably used to store textiles and, if the identification suggested below is correct, it contained specimens of papyrus flower.

The museum possesses a second box of the same man and other items of his are now in collections in Bologna, Leiden and the British Museum. These were almost certainly removed from a now-lost tomb in western Thebes, probably plundered in the rush for antiquities at the beginning of the 19th century. It is likely that it was at this stage that the boxes were opened and their contents, probably bedding or clothing, were removed.

These two boxes may almost certainly be identified with two which were purchased by Lord Prudhoe at the sale of Egyptian antiquities collected by Henry Salt in 1835. This box is described as 'well preserved and very fine, painted over with figures and hieroglyphics and containing in the inside specimens of the flower of papyrus, dried, exceedingly interesting.'

John Ruffle

47

Girl Carrying a Vase

Boxwood, ivory, black paint, and gold foil (base probably added in the 19th century CE); height (excluding mount) 13.3cm

Egypt, from the West Bank at Thebes
New Kingdom, 18th Dynasty, probably reign of Amenhotep III, about 1390–1350 BCE

Northumberland Collection
EG 4007

This beautiful object is both a statuette of a girl and a container, probably for a cosmetic oil or paste. It is a small masterpiece of inventive composition, showing the girl holding the jar on her left hip while making it usable without causing undue problems of stability. The jar is of a size suitable for actual use, not at the scale of a cosmetic vessel that the girl might hold. Instead she is shown as carrying a large and heavy object that affects her body pose accordingly. The artist achieved an extraordinary balance both in her figure and in the sculpture as a whole, as can be seen particularly in the view from above. He also made sure that the piece could be approached from any angle: the composition remains coherent and elegant as the eye travels all around it.

The girl is shown as pubescent, with a high waist and broadening hips but without developed breasts. An amulet of the familiar god Bes hangs from a necklace that is tied by a cord with trailing ends at the nape of the neck. At hip height she wears a girdle, originally gilded, that defines and offsets her pubic hair. At the back the girdle is at mid-buttock level, while above the buttocks are two dimples suggestive of a flesh covering and perhaps of movement.

Side views of the piece are remarkable. The pose is an adaptation of the standard position of moving female figures, with the left leg forward; it may also evoke the association of an adult woman balancing a baby on her left hip. The right leg, which is most unusually bent at the knee, forms a vertical with the torso and the head, but the backward shift of the left shoulder and forward lowering of the right shoulder combine to retain the sense of movement. The head, which appears to face straight ahead in a photograph taken from the front, can be seen from the side to be held at a very slight downward angle.

The lid of the jar is held in place by an ivory pin (a second pin is missing). The left ear is pierced, and a fragment of ivory behind it may have been part of an earring. Two holes drilled in the head were presumably for attaching hair, probably made in a black wood, which would have affected the appearance considerably.

The figure has been suggested to represent a Nubian or other foreigner, but nothing points toward any particular ethnic type. Figures of largely or completely nude girls in paintings, notably dancers shown in banquet scenes, are comparable in general appearance and never have any non-Egyptian features or identifying elements. It is simplest to see her as an Egyptian adolescent servant.

This is one of just a few pieces of ancient Egyptian statuary that depart radically from forms which face forward and stand or sit upright, so that their bodies are defined by axes intersecting roughly at right angles. The exceptional pieces are mostly in wood and date to the 18th dynasty, especially the reign of Amenhotep III (about 1391–1353 BCE), a time when vast numbers of small luxury objects were created. Many of these were discovered in tombs at Thebes by locals in the early 19th century and sold to visiting collectors, dealers, and amateurs. The Durham girl was probably acquired in this way by the future Duke of Northumberland, at about the same time as a couple of other pieces in major museums that became known from the 1920s onward. These works, among which the present piece is the finest and best preserved, have a more general importance for understanding Egyptian sculptural forms because they sharpen one's eyes when looking at larger and more seemingly rigid pieces. Detailed study shows that many statues of high quality, including ones in hard stones, subtly render accommodation of the body to temporary poses and other departures from an axial framework. Relatively very little statuary is preserved in wood, which encourages freer approaches than

stone; no doubt many more pieces that displayed these nuances existed than can now be estimated.

Thus, in addition to the unique qualities of this piece of small-scale sculpture, it has a wider significance in the study of Egyptian art and of how it is compared with other artistic traditions. The Oriental Museum is indeed fortunate to have this exceptional work in its collection.

John Baines

48

Kneeling Statue of the Vizier Paser

Granodiorite; height 80cm, width 27cm, depth 38cm

Egypt
New Kingdom, 19th Dynasty, reign of Ramesses II, about 1275 BCE

Northumberland Collection
EG4003

Power, piety and prestige emanate from the statue of Paser, the Vizier and Mayor of Thebes from the reign of Seti I to Ramesses II, about 1296–1260 BCE. The image shows him humbly kneeling and holding a now headless statuette of the god Ptah. Paser wears a long apron-like garment covering his body and tied at the back in a knot, to show his high office. His elaborate wig has long strands of crimped hair at the front framing the face and is covered by a second layer of rows of tight curls. His short, stylish beard and fashionable earrings also allude to his high status.

The hard igneous granodiorite of the statue is flecked with rusty and lighter coloured crystalline pieces, creating interesting contrasts of colour and light on the alternately polished (main body) and rough (inscriptions and wig) surfaces of the stone. The skill of the carving of such a hard stone, especially in the detail of the wig, show that the statue was made by the best craftsmen in Egypt and it is no accident that the god held by Paser was responsible for craftwork and craftsmen of all kinds. In fact, the statue was once dedicated at Memphis in the great temple of Ptah, a long way from the home of Paser in the south of Egypt. The statue therefore acted as a kind of substitute for Paser when he himself could not be present.

The inscription on the front of the statue reads:

'A gift which the king gives (and) Ptah, south of his wall, Lord of Ankh-Tawy. "May you make my body **strong** when raising up your perfection, my arms *carrying* your majesty every day; for my name is '*men*-**rudj**' or '*Firm* and **Strong**' in your temple." For the ka of the hereditary prince, Judge, Mouth of Nekhen, priest of Maat, Overseer of The City (Thebes), Vizier, Paser, true of voice.'

The italicised and bold words reflect the punning on two Egyptian words: *mn* 'firmness' and **rudj** 'strong' in the short text. It is possible that Paser, a man of no mean ability, composed the inscription himself.

Paser is known from documents, other stone monuments and his tomb at Thebes. He seems to have been extremely efficient and highly trusted by the kings Seti I and Ramesses II, as he would have been responsible for the area where the tombs of the king and his family were situated. The king himself would have been more involved in the north in his capital city of Pi-Ramesses and in the administrative centre at Memphis. Intended to be viewed from the front, the statue is a masterpiece of Ancient Egyptian civilization. Its apparent simplicity and power contrast with the immense investment of time, skill and effort in the creation of an ideal individual, designed to last for eternity.

Penny Wilson

49

Cat Mummy Case

Bronze; height 42cm

Egypt
Late Period, 26th Dynasty, about 600 BCE

Northumberland Collection
EG5082

This life-size hollow bronze cat mummy case dates to around the 26th Dynasty of the Late Period of Ancient Egyptian history (about 600 BCE). It came to the Oriental Museum as part of the Alnwick Collection bought by Durham University from the Duke of Northumberland in the 1950s. On its arrival at the Oriental Museum the statuette contained a poorly preserved cat mummy, which unfortunately has since been lost.

The cat had religious significance throughout Egyptian history and was especially important during the Late Period when there was a considerable increase in the number of animal cults. Egyptian cats were particularly linked with the goddess Bastet, a female cat deity representing maternal qualities, but were also associated with more volatile goddesses such as Sekhmet, who took the form of a ferocious lioness. As such, the cat itself became a focus of worship as a manifestation of these divine beings. Towns with strong connections to Bastet and feline deities, for example Speos Artemidos in Middle Egypt and Tell Basta (Bubastis) in the East Delta in the North East of Egypt, were home to temples and festivals dedicated to the cat goddess. Bubastis was the main centre of the cat cult during the Late Period.

On the day of the Festival of Bastet, thousands of people would flock to Bubastis to give thanks for good fortune and to pray for advice and help at the temple. An important part of worship in animal cults was to give an offering to the gods. At Tuna el-Gebel in Middle Egypt this resulted in the mummification and burial of hundreds of thousands of baboons and ibis associated with the god Thoth. At Bubastis, thousands upon thousands of cats were mummified and offered to Bastet. Specialist temples such as that at Bubastis had catteries attached to them which offered a ready supply of cats to be used in such rituals. There is evidence that in preparation for festivals and pilgrimages animals from these catteries were sacrificed and mummified in preparation for the upcoming high demand.

During these festivals or pilgrimages anybody could purchase a cat mummy and/or statuette and have it dedicated as an offering to the goddess. The offerings varied from the very cheap and crudely made to expensive and elaborate mummies and figurines. Not everything was always as it seemed, and some 'mummies' were forgeries containing only a few cat bones or even no animal material at all! After they had been offered to Bastet, the cat mummies were deposited in specially made mass graves or in an animal necropolis. This bronze statuette was probably utilised in a similar context and is quite unusual in that it was made as a case for a cat mummy, which could be inserted through a hole in the base; most cat figurines were far too small to hold any animal. The care and detail put into this piece fittingly reflects the respect and esteem allotted to the ancient Egyptian cat and its divine relations.

Kathryn Jacques

50

Oil Lamp of the Patriarch Timothy II

Terracotta; length 12cm

Egypt
5th century CE

Northumberland Collection
EG6785

Whilst limestone and crude ceramic lamps were in widespread use under the Pharaohs, it was not until after the conquest of Alexander the Great that mould-made ceramic lamps began to be imported into Egypt. During the Roman period moulded ceramic lamps began to be mass-produced and distinctive Egyptian types rapidly evolved. Oil lamps produced in Egypt during the Roman period were often decorated with images of frogs or toads; a reference to the Egyptian deity Heket, who was associated with the renewal of life and childbirth. The use of the symbolic frog continued into the Christian period, when it was adopted as a symbol of the Resurrection. The frog motif appears prominently on an exceptional Christian lamp in the Oriental Museum collection. The lamp also bears the inscription, ABBA TIMOΘEOY APXIEΠICKOΠ, which may be translated as 'of father Timotheos, the Archbishop'.

The inscription is likely to be a reference to Timothy II, the Coptic Pope of Alexandria (457–477 CE) who served as a figurehead for the many Egyptian clerics who opposed the Chalcedonian interpretation of the nature of Christ which had been imposed upon their homeland by the Byzantine emperor. Timothy, who was also known as Aelurus (the Weasel) because of his small stature, was banished from Alexandria in 459 CE. He spent many years in exile at Gangra, where he wrote a series of *Canonical Responses* and a work entitled *Against Chalcedon* but,

upon returning to Alexandria following a rebellion in 475 CE, was re-established as Patriarch.

The lamp was formerly in the collection of the Dukes of Northumberland at Alnwick Castle. Its exceptional quality and significance attracted the attention of the North Eastern antiquarian Robert Coltman Clephan FSA, who described it in detail in his pioneering work on ancient oil lamps.

Craig Barclay

Bibliography and Further Reading

1   Chinese Archery

Selby, Stephen, 2000. *Chinese Archery*. Aberdeen (HK): Hong Kong University.

2   Terracotta Tang Dynasty Polo Player

Legeza, Ireneus Laszlo, 1972. *A Descriptive Catalogue of the Malcolm MacDonald Collection of Chinese Ceramics*. London: Oxford University Press.

3   Song Dynasty Bowl with Mandarin Duck Design

Legeza, Ireneus Laszlo, 1972. *A Descriptive Catalogue of the Malcolm MacDonald Collection of Chinese Ceramics*. London: Oxford University Press.

Li, He, 1996. *Chinese Ceramics: the New Standard Guide*. London: Thames and Hudson.

4   Shu Fu Porcelain Stem Cup with Dragon Design

Legeza, Ireneus Laszlo, 1972. *A Descriptive Catalogue of the Malcolm MacDonald Collection of Chinese Ceramics*. London: Oxford University Press.

Li, He, 1996. *Chinese Ceramics: the New Standard Guide*. London: Thames and Hudson.

5   Rhinoceros Horn Libation Cup

Anon., 2000. *Selected Chinese Art from the Oriental Museum, Durham*. London: Phillips.

Chapman, Jan, 1999. *The Art of Rhinoceros Horn Carving in China*. London: Christies.

6   Eight Album Leaves Attributed to Gong Xian (1618–89)

Cahill, James, 1982. *The Compelling Image: Nature and Style in Seventeenth-Century Chinese Painting*. Cambridge (MA): Harvard University Press.

Silbergeld, Jerome, 1981. 'Kung Hsien: A Professional Chinese Artist and His Patronage' in *The Burlington Magazine*, vol.123 no.940, pp. 400–410.

Smith, Judith G. & Wen C. Fong, 1999. *Issues of Authenticity in Chinese Painting*. New York: The Metropolitan Museum of Art.

Watson, William & Chuimei Ho, 2007. *The Arts of China After 1620*. New Haven & London: Yale University Press.

8   Astronomical Clock

Pan Nai (ed.), 2005. *The History of Ancient Astronomical Instruments in China, Shanxi*. (In Chinese).

Stephenson, F.R., 1994. 'Chinese and Korean Star Maps and Catalogs', in *Cartography in the Traditional East and Southeast Asian Societies: The History of Cartography*, vol., 2, book 2, pp. 511–578.

10   Embroidered Dragon Robe

Vainker, Shelagh, 2004. *Chinese Silk: a Cultural History*. London, British Museum Press.

11   Export Paintings on Pith

Williams, Ifan, 2008. *Chinese Paintings on Pith at the National Arts Club, 15 Gramercy Park, South New York, 8th to 15th June 2008*. Private publication.

12   Chao Mei and his *Autumn Glory*

Farrer, A., 2003. *Chinese Printmaking Today: Woodblock Printing in China 1980–2000*, London: British Library.

von der Burg, Christer, 2003. *The Art of Contemporary Chinese Woodcuts*. London: Muban Foundation.

13   Thangka Showing the Goddess Green Tara

1961. 'Marquess of Zetland: Proconsul and Author', obituary, *The Times*, 7 Feb., p.13

Harris, Clare, 1999. *In the Image of Tibet: Tibetan Painting after 1959*. Reaktion.

Jackson, David P. and Janice A. Jackson, 1984. *Tibetan Thangka Painting: Methods and Manners*. London: Serindia.

Willis, Michael, 1999. *Tibet: Life, Myth and Art*. London: Duncan Baird Publishers, p. 78.

Woods, Philip, 2004. 'Dundas, Lawrence John Lumley, Second Marquess of Zetland (1876–1961)', *Oxford Dictionary of National Biography*, Oxford University Press, Sept 2004; online edn, May 2009. Available at: http://www.oxforddnb.com/view/article/32932 (Accessed December 2009)

14   Human Skull-cup

Guidelines on Policy for Human Remains in Surrey Museums www.surreymuseums.org.uk/working/PolicyOnHumanRemains.pdf (*December 2009*)

2005. *Guidance for the Care of Human Remains in Museums*. London, Department for Culture, Media and Sport.

15 Prayer Wheel
Martin, Dan, 1987. 'On the Origin and Significance of the Prayer Wheel, According to two Nineteenth-century Tibetan Literary Sources', in *Journal of the Tibet Society*, vol. 7, pp. 13–29.
Reynolds, Valrae, 1999. *From the Sacred Realm: Treasures of Tibetan Art from the Newark Museum*. Munich, London, New York: Prestel, p. 55.
Willis, Michael, 1999. *Tibet: Life, Myth and Art*. London: Duncan Baird Publishers, p. 78.
Zaleski, Philip and Zaleski, Carol, 2005. *Prayer: A History*. New York: Houghton Mifflin Harcourt, pp. 3–4.

16 Monk's Rice Bowl
McArthur, Meher, 2002. *Reading Buddhist Art: An Illustrated Guide to Buddhist Signs and Symbols*. London: Thames & Hudson.
Oxford English Dictionary [Online]. Available at: http://dictionary.oed.com (Accessed December 2009)

19 The Durham Bodhisattva
Ali, I. & Coningham, R.A.E. 2002. 'Recording and Preserving Gandhara's Cultural Heritage', in Brodie J., Doole J. & Renfrew A.C. (eds.) *Illicit Antiquities: the Destruction of the World's Archaeological Heritage*. Cambridge: McDonald Institute for Archaeological Research, pp. 25–31.
Coningham. R.A.E. & Manuel, M.J. 2009. 'Great Empires of South Asia', in Harrison, T. (ed.) *The Great Empires of the Ancient World*. London: Thames & Hudson, pp. 226–249.
Cribb, J. & Errington, E. 1992. *The Crossroads of Asia: Transformation in Image and Symbol*. Cambridge: Ancient India & Iran Trust.
Nehru, L. 1989. *The Origins of The Gandharan Style: A Study Of Contributory Influences*. Oxford: Oxford University Press.
Zwalf, W. 1996. *A Catalogue of the Gandhara Sculpture in the British Museum*. London: British Museum Press.

22 Jewelled Necklace
2005. 'Professor Helen Muir' (Obituary), *Daily Telegraph*, 15 Dec.
2006. 'Helen Muir' (Obituary), *The Guardian* 4 Jan.

25 Shino Ware Tea-bowl
Wilson, Richard L., 2005. *Inside Japanese Ceramics*. New York and Tokyo: Weatherhill.
Sanders, Herbert, *The World of Japanese Ceramics*. Kodansha, Tokyo & Palo Alto: Kodansha.

27 Hiroshige Woodblock Print
Uspensky, Mikhail, 2005. *Hiroshige One Hundred Views of Edo*. New York: Barnes & Noble.

29 Burmese Manuscript Chest
Khur-yearn, J. 2007, 'Richness of Buddhist Texts in Shan Manuscripts: A report of work in progress on the Seven Shan Versions of Satipatthaana Sutta'. Unpublished conference paper.
Rawson, P., 1967. *The Art of Southeast Asia*. London: Thames & Hudson. pp. 198–200.
Terwiel, B.J., 2003, *Shan Manuscripts Vol. 1*. Stuttgart: F. Steiner.

30 Iban Headhunting Sword
Macdonald, Malcolm (The Rt. Hon.), 1972. *Borneo People*. London: Jonathan Cape.
Ritchie, James, 1999. *The life story of Temenggong Koh, 1870–1956*. Kuching: Kacha Holdings.

32 Carved Wooden Panel Showing Scenes from the Ramayana
Losty, J. P., 2008. *The Ramayana: Love and Valour in India's Great Epic*. London: British Library Publishing.

33 Barrel Cylinder of Nebuchadnezzar II
Berger, P.-R., 1973. *Die Neubabylonischen Königsinschriften*. Neukirchen-Vluyn
Bogenaar, A.C.V.M., 1997. *The Neo-Babylonian Ebabbar Temple at Sippar: its Administration and its Prosopography*. Istanbul.
Langdon, S., 1912. *Die Neubabylonischen Königsinschriften*, trans. R. Zehnpfund. Leipzig: Hinrichs.
Schaudig, H.-P., 2001. *Die Inschriften Nabonids von Babylon und Kyros' des Grossen: Textausgabe und Grammatik*. Münster.
Wiseman, D.J., 1985. *Nebuchadnezzar and Babylon*, London: Oxford University Press.

34 Carved Stone Relief from the Palace of Ashurbanipal at Nineveh
Barnett, R.D., 1976. *Sculptures from the North Palace of Ashurbanipal at Nineveh (668–627 BC)*. London, British Museum Publications.

36 Mina'i Ware Bowl
Allan, J.T., 1973. 'Ab 'l-Q sim's Treatise on Ceramics', in *Iran* 11, pp. 111–120.
Ettinghausen, R., 1970. 'The Flowering of Seljuq Art'. *Metropolitan Museum of Art Journal* 3, pp. 113–131.
Jenkins, M., 1983. 'Islamic Pottery: A Brief History'. *Metropolitan Museum of Art Bulletin* 40/4, pp. 1–52.
Manners, E., 1990. *Ceramics Sourcebook: A Visual Guide to the*

World's Great Ceramic Traditions. London: Collins & Brown.

Mason, R., 1997. 'Medieval Iranian Lustre-Painted and Associated Wares: Typology in a Multidisciplinary Study', in *Iran* 35, pp. 103–135.

37 Islamic Calligraphy

Anon. *Islamic Calligraphy*. Wikipedia. Available at: http://en.wikipedia.org/wiki/Islamic_calligraphy

http://en.wikipedia.org/wiki/Islamic_calligraphy#cite_note-Bloom_1999.2C_pg._218-0

The Applied History Research Group, 1998. *The Islamic World to 1600; Calligraphy*. [Online]. University of Calgary. Available at: http://www.ucalgary.ca/applied_history/tutor/islam/learning/calligraphy.html (Accessed December 2009)

Imam Reza (A.S.) Network. *Calligraphy: The Unifying Characteristic of the Islamic Art*. [Online]. Available at: http://www.imamreza.net/eng/imamreza.php?id=631 (Accessed December 2009)

Anon., 1983. 'The Islamic Collection' in *Arts of Asia*, vol.13, no. 6, pp. 88–89.

38 Heb-Sed Vessel Pepi II

Goebs, Katja, 2010. 'Kingship', in Wilkinson, T. (ed.) *The Egyptian World*. Abingdon, ch. 20.

Hardwick, Tom, 2008, in Reeves, N. (ed.), *Egyptian Art at Eton College and Durham University*, Tokyo: Tokyo Shimbun, p. 150, cat. no. 202.

Wilkinson, Toby, 2007. *Lives of the Ancient Egyptians*. London, no. 20.

39 Stela of Dedu

Birch, Samuel, 1880. *Catalogue of the Collection of the Egyptian Antiquities at Alnwick Castle*. London: R. Clay Sons and Taylor, pp. 264–6, Cat. no. 1932.

O'Connor, D., 1985. 'The "Cenotaphs" of the Middle Kingdom at Abydos,' in Psener-Kriéger, P (ed.) *Mélanges Gamal Eddin Mokhtar*. Cairo: Institut Français d'Archéologie Orientale, pp. 161–178.

O'Connor, D., 2009. *Abydos. Egypt's First Pharaohs and the Cult of Osiris*. London: Thames and Hudson (New Aspects of Antiquity).

Richards, J., 2005. *Society and Death in Ancient Egypt. Mortuary Landscapes of the Middle Kingdom*. Cambridge: Cambridge University Press.

Ruffle, John, 2008, in Reeves, N. (ed.), *Egyptian Art at Eton College and Durham University*., Tokyo: Tokyo Shimbun, pp. 134–5, cat. no. 178.

Simpson, W.K., 1974. *The Terrace of the Great God at Abydos: The Offering Chapels of Dynasties 12 and 13*. New Haven: Peabody Museum of Natural History.

40 Trussed and Plucked Duck Vessel

Bourriau, J.D., 1988. *Pharaohs and Mortals*, Egyptian Art in the Middle Kingdom. Cambridge: Cambridge University Press, p.141, no. 143.

Hardwick, Tom, 2008, in Reeves, N. (ed.), *Egyptian Art at Eton College and Durham University*. Tokyo: Tokyo Shimbun, p. 181, cat. no. 251.

Nicholson, P.T. and Shaw, I.E. 2000. *Ancient Egyptian Materials and Technology*. Cambridge: Cambridge University Press.

Peet, T.E. 1914. *Cemeteries of Abydos*, II. London: pl. XIII, 14.

Terrace, E.B.1966. 'Blue Marble' Plastic Vessels, *Journal of the American Research Center in Egypt 5*, pp. 57–68.

41 Funerary Mask

Dodson, A., 1998. 'A Funerary Mask in Durham and mummy adornment in the late Second Intermediate Period and early Eighteenth Dynasty', in *Journal of Egyptian Archaeology* 84, pp. 93–9.

Hardwick, Tom, 2008, in Reeves, N. (ed.), *Egyptian Art at Eton College and Durham University*. Tokyo: Tokyo Shimbun, p. 155, cat. no. 210.

42 Jar Inscribed for Queen Hatshepsut

Hardwick, Tom, 2008, in Reeves, N. (ed.), *Egyptian Art at Eton College and Durham University*. Tokyo: Tokyo Shimbun, p. 68, cat. no. 63.

Robins G., 1993. *Women in Ancient Egypt*. London: British Museum Press.

Roehrig, C. (ed.), 2005. *Hatshepsut from Queen to Pharaoh*. Yale: Yale University Press.

Shaw, I. (ed.), 2000. *The Oxford History of Ancient Egypt*. Oxford: Oxford University Press.

Troy, L. 1986. *Patterns of Queenship in Ancient Egyptian Myth and History (*Acta Universitatis Upsaliensis 14). Uppsala: Universitetet.

43 Shabti of Prince Bahmery

Schneider, Hans D., 1977. *Shabtis, An Introduction to the History of Ancient Egyptian Funerary Statuettes*, 3 vols. Leiden.

Schneider, Hans D., 2008, in Reeves, N. (ed.), *Egyptian Art at Eton College and Durham University*. Tokyo: Tokyo Shimbun, p. 144, cat. no. 191.

Stewart, Harry M., 1995. *Egyptian Shabtis*. Princes Risborough: Shire.

45 Sphinx of Tuthmosis IV

Birch, Samuel, 1880. *Catalogue of the Collection of Egyptian Antiquities at Alnwick Castle*. London: Clay & Taylor, pp. 42–3, cat. no. 379.

Schneider, Hans D., 2008, in Reeves, N. (ed.), *Egyptian Art at Eton College and Durham University.* Tokyo: Tokyo Shimbun, p. 187, cat. no. 255.

Malek, J., 1999. *Egyptian Art.* Phaidon Press.

Wilkinson, Richard, H., 1994. *Reading Egyptian Art.* London: Thames and Hudson.

46 Decorated Box of Perpauty and his Wife Ady

Catalogue of the Highly Interesting and Magnificent Collection of Egyptian Antiquities, the Property of the Late Henry Salt Esq. His Britannic Majesty's Late Consul General in Egypt. June 1835, lot 25.

Birch, S., 1880. *Catalogue of the Collection of Egyptian Antiquities at Alnwick Castle.* London: Clay & Taylor, pp. 193–196, cat. no. 1459.

Harris, J.R., 1983. 'Some Well Known Egyptian Pieces Reconsidered', *Arts of Asia* vol.13, no. 6, pp. 76–8, fig. 22.

Kozloff, A.P., 1993, in Kosloff et. Al. (eds.) *Amenophis III, Le Pharaon-Soleil.* Paris, pp. 250–52, cat. no. 53.

Ruffle, John, 2008, in Reeves, N. (ed.), *Egyptian Art at Eton College and Durham University.* Tokyo: Tokyo Shimbun, pp.100–101, cat. no. 115.

47 Girl Carrying a Vase

Birch, Samuel, 1880. *Catalogue of the Collection of Egyptian Antiquities at Alnwick Castle.* London: Clay & Taylor, p. 99, cat. no. 752.

Capart, Jean, 1923. 'L'art Egyptien et la Loi de Frontalité: à Propos d'une Statuette du Cabinet des Médailles', *Fondation Eugène Piot, Monuments et Mémoires* 26, pp. 47–65.

Harris, J. R., 1983. 'Some Well Known Egyptian Pieces Reconsidered', in *Arts of Asia,* vol. 13, no.6, p. 79.

Kozloff, A.P., 1992, in Kozloff, A.P., Bryan, B.M. & Berman, L.M (eds.) *Egypt's Dazzling Sun: Amenhotep III and His World,* Exhibition catalogue. Cleveland: Cleveland Museum of Art; Indiana University Press, pp. 361–2, cat. no. 87.

Schäfer, Heinrich, 1963. *Principles of Egyptian Art.* 4th Edition. Brunner-Traut, Emma (ed.), translated from German by Baines, John (ed.). Oxford: Griffith Institute, p. 318 & no.15.

Schneider, Hans D., 2008, in Reeves, N. (ed.), *Egyptian Art at Eton College and Durham University.* Tokyo: Tokyo Shimbun, p. 189, cat. no. 261.

48 Kneeling Statue of the Vizier Paser

Helck, W., 1958. *Zur Verwaltung des Mittleren und Neuen Reichs.* Brill: Leiden-Köln.

Kitchen, K.A., 1988. *Pharaoh Triumphant. The Life and Times of Ramesses II.* Warminster.

Hardwick, Tom, 2008, in Reeves, N. (ed.), *Egyptian Art at Eton College and Durham Universit.,* Tokyo: Tokyo Shimbun, p. 181, cat. no. 251.

Schneider, Hans D., 2008, in Reeves, N. (ed.), *Egyptian Art at Eton College and Durham University.* Tokyo: Tokyo Shimbun, p. 192, cat. no. 264.

49 Cat Mummy Case

Kemp, B., 2007. *Ancient Egypt; Anatomy of a Civilization,* 2nd Edition. Oxford: Routledge.

Lloyd, A.B., 2003. 'The Late Period (664–332 BC)', in Shaw, I. (ed.), *The Oxford History of Ancient History.* Oxford: Oxford University Press, pp. 364–387.

Malek, J., 1997. *The Cat in Ancient Egypt.* London: British Museum Press.

Pinch, G., 2004. *Egyptian Mythology; A Guide to the Gods, Goddesses, and Traditions of Ancient Egypt.* Oxford: Oxford University Press.

Schneider, Hans D., 2008, in Reeves, N. (ed.), *Egyptian Art at Eton College and Durham University.* Tokyo: Tokyo Shimbun, p. 54, cat. no. 36.

50 Oil Lamp of Patriarch Timothy II

Cannuyer, Christian, 2001. *Coptic Egypt: the Christians of the Nile.* London: Thames & Hudson.

Clephan, Robert Coltman, 1906–7. 'On Terra-cotta Lamps', in *Proceedings of the Society of Antiquaries of Scotland* 41, pp. 34–62.

Birch, Samuel, 1880. *Catalogue of the Collection of Egyptian Antiquities at Alnwick Castle.* London: Clay & Taylor.

Overleaf: Ancient Egyptian statuette of a girl carrying a vase (no. 47).

North.
752.